From Doubt to Defense

Acts as the Key to Confident Faith

The Book of Acts is a template for understanding & effectively sharing your faith.

Suitable for Sunday school or home Bible study use, teens and adults.

Compiled & written by Ronald Parrs

Copyright Information

Scripture quotations are from the ESV® Bible (The Holy Bible, English Standard Version®), © 2001 by Crossway, a publishing ministry of Good News Publishers. Used by permission. All rights reserved. The ESV text may not be quoted in any publication made available to the public by a Creative Commons license. The ESV may not be translated in whole or in part into any other language.

Copyright © 2025 Ronald Parrs

All rights reserved.

No part of this publication may be reproduced, distributed, or transmitted in any form or by any means, including photocopying, recording or other electronic or mechanical methods, without the prior written permission of the publisher except as permitted by U.S. copyright law.

Certain preexisting materials such as artwork and photographs are included with the appropriate original source noted and credited if available.

Table of Contents

Dedication 5
Disclaimer 6
Preface & Acknowledgements 7
From Doubt to Defense – an Overview 11
What is the Book of Acts Really About? 15
Lesson 1 - Why Christian Theism? 19
Lesson 2 – Who is God 29
Lesson 3 - Getting Started Requires a Good Start 41
Lesson 4 - Speaking in Tongues 49
Spiritual Gifts 57
Lesson 5 - Peter's Keys to Apologetics 67
Follow Peter's Example... 77
Continue to Follow Peter's Example 83
The Unbelieving Mind 89
Lesson 6 - Practical Preaching 95
Lesson 7 - Right Relationship 101
Lesson 8 - The Sin Problem 111
Dignity and Depravity 119
Lesson 9 - The Redemption Solution 129
Lesson 10 - A Christian Worldview, part 1 137
A Christian Worldview, part 2 143
A Worldview Example 151
Lesson 11 - The Unbeliever's Worldview 157
The Gospel vs. the Hamster Wheel of the "isms" 167
Lesson 12 - Actions and Attitudes 175
Lesson 13 - Apologetic Strategies 181
Lesson 14 – Wrapping it Up and Back to Basics 191
Key Verses & Passages 197
Resources 199

Appendix – Study Leader Notes 201

Dedication

From Doubt to Defense is a Bible study dedicated to the hundreds of thousands of men and women who, for almost 2000 years, have chosen to make the time to proclaim their love of God openly. In so doing, they have obeyed the call of proclaiming the Gospel as Jesus instructed in Matthew 28. These men and women did so in the face of adversity and extreme persecution to the point of imprisonment and even death. In their trials, they allowed the Holy Spirit to speak through them, bringing hope of Salvation and eternal life with God to a world that is dying in sin yet has a loving and merciful God Who is eager to restore the relationship as it was in the Garden before the Fall. As we proclaim Jesus's Saving work on the Cross and His glorious Resurrection, each of us who has accepted His free gift of Salvation has a story to tell – our personal apologetic – as a witness to bring others to the same saving knowledge of Christ and to live with Him eternally.

Disclaimer

Unless otherwise stated, all site content (text, image files created and/or owned by the site, etc.) is Copyright © Ronald Parrs (and the site owner and author), all rights reserved.

Any materials are strictly offered for informational and educational purposes and personal use only and is not and should not be considered professional advice on any given topic or subject (e.g. medical and mental conditions, legal advice, etc.). Site content and any correspondence exchanged with the author should not replace professional advice by qualified entities.

Preface & Acknowledgements

From Doubt to Defense is a Bible study of the convergence of several events. With God, nothing is "coincidental". I had been listening to and studying a sermon series on defending the Christian Faith. It was fascinating. I listened to it over and over. I took copious mental as well as written notes. My personal study continued for several months. The men's Bible study community group I have been meeting with on Saturday mornings for the past two decades was about to begin afresh after the summer's hiatus. We discussed what we would study. I was "pushing" a study of Apologetics. One of our group's members really wanted to study the Book of Acts. So, I said, "Sure, we could blend these two ideas into a comprehensive Bible study. This will be fun!"

As I left the group that morning, I thought, "Lord, help me! Open my eyes to Your Word and work in my mind." And that's precisely what God did. Thanks to the members of this study group. God has used this time to sharpen each one of us in so many ways.

What are my credentials? I don't have any. I have no college or university degrees in Theology. I am not a pastor or an apologist. God has blessed me with the gift of teaching and counseling. One of my passions is opening up and exploring the Bible and its Truths for my own study and with others. I have been a senior high school and adult Sunday school teacher at my home church since the mid-1990s. When tasked with teaching a particular topic or book of the Bible, my mission is to sit down and write a complete study from introduction to conclusion, providing context and study tools to my charges as to what we were studying.

This study is specifically meant for the student or layperson, regardless of age, who has had no formal training in apologetics or theology. This study is designed just for you. You discovered *From Doubt to Defense* because you desire to grow in your Christian faith and grasp a better understanding of why you believe what you believe about God, the Bible, and even yourself. You also want to know how to best speak to others, especially non-believers, about your faith in Jesus.

As Paul writes in 2 Timothy 2:14-16, *[14] Remind them of these things, and charge them before God not to quarrel about words, which does no good, but only ruins the hearers. [15] Do your best to present yourself to God as one approved, a worker who has no need to be ashamed, rightly handling the word of truth. ¹⁶ But avoid irreverent babble, for it will lead people into more and more ungodliness,* we are to know and articulate God's Word and His Truths.

But what about the title, *From Doubt to Defense*? Is there a reason for that particular title? Yes, there is a reason. I've been struggling with getting a proper attention-grabbing title. As I prayed over the list of titles my pastor friend Abel gave me, the Holy Spirit brought up image after image of faith-filled believers from the Old Testament (pre-Christians) and New Testament. From Adam to Noah to Job to Abraham and the other patriarchs, then Moses and other prophets, even Esther; then onto John the Baptist, Peter, Paul, and up to today, every one of these people was at one time or another subject to a crossroad in their life. At the crossroads, there are only two signs: hear God's call, trust what He will do and move forward in obedience, or ignore the call, don't trust and obey, and go your own way.

At the crossroads of life, there is confusion and doubt. There are typically no "clear" answers or directions. But on one of those roads, there is likely one small point of the light of hope. As we follow the road toward hope, we are now able to defend the direction we are headed in, hence the title *From Doubt to Defense*.

We are at a critical crossroads in human history. Many individuals and institutions want to silence the Church, its people, and most importantly, God's Word itself because it doesn't – and won't – align with the current zeitgeist (spirit of the age). God has called each of us to speak His Gospel. Amazingly, although there is more suppression, there is an outpouring of God's Spirit in many parts of the world that are otherwise closed. Quoting Jesus, "*I will build my church, and the gates of hell shall not prevail against it.*"

God has called and is using each of us to further His Gospel every day and with as many people as we may encounter. Now, how can we best proceed?

There are three thematic verses that form the foundation or the "why" of this Study. 1 Peter 3:15 – 16, admonishes us to be always prepared to give a reason to unbelievers (or pre-believers, if you will) for our hope in Christ. Furthermore, we are to give that reason for hope with gentleness and humility, but more importantly, with the power of the Holy Spirit. The purpose is to help lead others to a saving knowledge of Jesus Christ. The other two passages are 2 Peter 3:15 - 18, which helps us to understand what we are up against as we defend our faith, and Romans 1:18 - 32, which allows us to understand the decaying state of the unbeliever and why they are in a continuing downward spiral.

With each lesson (not necessarily the chapters), you'll find a study sheet to use with your class or small group to stimulate conversation.

So, we turn to the Study of *From Doubt to Defense*. My great thanks go to Pastor Brian Borgman of Grace Community Church of Minden, Nevada, and his sermon series "Defense of Christian Theism," which was the seed of this study. Several other resources were used and are noted in the resource guide found on the Resources page.

A special thanks to my friend of many years Pastor Abel Arias (M.Div., Ph.D. candidate, Bible Exposition) for his editorial help and biblical feedback.

A giant thankyou to my dear friend and graphic artist Connie Hovan for her work on cover design. Connie unveiled (again) exactly what was needed to convey the sentiment and feel of the book. I'm always grateful for her efforts.

Thank you to my new and dear friend, Veronica Taveras, Executive Director of The Bienvenido Project in the Dominican Republic, who assisted in editing the Spanish version and clarifying many idiomatic expressions.

Thanks to my church's youth pastor at the time, Michael Kraft, who asked me one Sunday to come alongside him to teach in the High School Sunday School class. "Ron, do you have anything?" "Yes! A study on apologetics." We started with eight weeks of prepared content and ended up going twelve weeks as the students kept wanting more!

I also want to thank some personal friends and mentors (you know who you are) who have stood by to lovingly critique this work and "harden" some of the soft ideas as well as soften some of the "hard" ideas. Thank you for your encouragement.

Finally, but primarily, I give thanks and praise to God my Father, who kept prompting my mind to action; Jesus the Son, who guarantees my eternal life as I've trusted Him as my Lord and Savior; and the Holy Spirit, who has been alive and working as He opens my eyes to His Truths and keeps my fingers typing my keyboard's keys.

From Doubt to Defense – an Overview

Learning about Apologetics using the Book of Acts gives practical insight into how we are to approach the world around us.

What is Apologetics? 1 Peter 3:15 instructs us to give a reason for the hope that we have in Christ and to be ready to always give a defense of the Gospel. And that means at ALL times by EVERY one of us. We are living in times alluded to in 2 Peter 3:15 - 18 which touches on the urgency and power with which we believers need to properly defend our Faith.

Over the weeks as you delve into this study, I believe you'll have some good stimulating discussions. It is my prayer that you'll come away with practical ideas of how to better present as well as represent Jesus Christ in you to your family, friends, neighbors, and strangers.

At the end of the book, you'll find a list of excellent resources from various Christian authors, going through foundational Biblical truths, exposing current "post-modern" and "post-Christian" thought and worldviews and how to properly defend YOUR faith.

Introduction. Here are some thoughts on the purpose behind this study using God's Word (the Book of Acts) to prepare yourself and your small group with the basics of Apologetics as we share our faith with other believers and nonbelievers as well. God call us to think deeply, using every resource He's given to spread the Gospel of Jesus Christ with clarity, purpose, and impact to a world that desperately needs Him.

What is Christian Theism? – Let's start by understanding what we're talking about.

Who is God? – We must build a firm foundation of Who He is and who we are.

From Doubt to Defense - Chapter 1 of the Book of Acts is packed with the basics of Apologetics and how Jesus Christ Himself, teaches us how to approach our world.

Speaking in Tongues – We will look at how Chapter 2 of the Book of Acts provides an insight as to how we should speak and what the Gospel message should be.

Spiritual Gifts – Speaking in tongues is just one of the many Spiritual Gifts that God the Holy Spirit gave to God's people in the early church. Each of these gifts is meant to be used to help advance God's Kingdom and to fulfill His plan.

Christ's Keys of Truth – In Chapter 2 of the Book of Acts, the Apostle Peter – a former Galilean fisherman – follows Jesus' instruction and boldly speaks. Empowered by the Holy Spirit, his words lead 3,000 people to faith in Christ.

Peter's Keys to Apologetics – Understanding 1 Peter 3:15-16

Follow Peter's Example – Understanding 2 Peter 3:14-18

The Unbelieving Mind – Why understanding the book of Romans, chapter one is critical in understanding the unbelievers around us.

Practicing what we Preach - Chapter 2 of the Book of Acts ends with a word picture of how this new community of believers were leading their lives and their impact on the surrounding neighborhood. That's very good - but what do we believers do with the Bible? How does the Bible relate to Apologetics?

Who and What is your foundation? – Each of us must have a solid foundation: Who is God and our relationship to Him? Do we know what we believe, and do we believe what we know? Let's stop and take a check of our own personal beliefs or as is called now, our Christian worldview.

The Sin Problem - Sin. That awful, three letter word. Chapter 7 of the Book of Acts details Stephen's incredible "apologia" to the Jewish Sanhedrin. Stephen knew that man needed a Savior and God had set the wheels in motion millennia earlier. He told the Truth and for that they took his life. What are the noetic effects of sin?

Dignity and Depravity – Christianity is the only religion or belief system that fully demonstrates mankind's divine dignity and utter depravity.

The Redemption Solution - Sin is ugly but the Redemption we have in Jesus Christ is Glorious! Redemption begins in the mind and then permeates through our entire being restoring our relationship to the way God had intended. Acts Chapter 8.

Defining a Worldview, Part 1 - What is a "worldview"? Everyone has one. What makes up a worldview and why it is important to understand as we formulate our apologetic. Born again, Bible believing Christians have a worldview. Do you understand yours? How do you not only express it but live it. The first three aspects of what constitutes a worldview.

Defining a Worldview, Part 2 – The fourth, fifth, sixth, and seventh aspects of what constitutes a person's worldview.

Non-Christian (unbeliever's) Worldview - The unbelieving worldview is radically different. In forming our apologetic, we must understand how they think and more importantly, why they think the way they do.

The Gospel vs. the Hamster Wheel of the "isms" – The Gospel of Jesus Christ is the good news for everyone, no matter their background, status or circumstances. God wants people to "come as they are" – He's here to heal, restore, redeem, and provide purpose in our lives. The Gospel offers true freedom for life and living in contrast to the endless cycle of striving and struggling without purpose – like running on a hamster wheel

Actions and Attitudes - Acts 11:1 - 18; 17:1 - 9; 23:1 - 10; 24:24 - 27. The myths of Neutrality and Autonomy. What is the Christian believer's attitudes and actions to be like when presenting our Apologetic?

Apologetic Strategies - Acts 25 - 26. Paul is standing before 2 leaders that "hold" his fate: the Roman Governor Festus and the Jewish King Agrippa. As we construct our own apologetic, we depend on God, His Word and His working in our lives. We remember that God is our Foundation as well as our Defense.

Final Thoughts - A few closing personal thoughts on the importance of Apologetics. Apologetics is not the be all, end all. We need to have a heart for the lost.

Key Verses & Passages – These thoughts form the foundation and framework for constructing your personal apologetic.

Resources – A listing of the various books and their authors used in this study.

Appendix – Study Leader notes for each lesson.

What is the Book of Acts Really About?

We think we know what the Book of Acts is all about... or maybe we don't.

Well, maybe. Sometimes it's known as the Book of the Acts of the Apostles authored by Luke, a Greek physician. But there's more to it than just that. It is the history book of the New Testament. Others have "renamed" it the Acts of the Holy Spirit. That idea has a lot of merit. As the Holy Spirit comes into or indwells all believers in Jesus Christ as part of the New Covenant of God, He, the Spirit, acts in and through us.

Now mention the word "apologetics" and most people's eyes glaze over. That happens, I believe, because we don't understand what apologetics is. They think it's something that requires years of seminary study or professional training. We think of today's "big name" evangelists such as Billy or Franklin Graham, Luis Palau or any number of radio and television pastors.

Strictly speaking, apologetics is simply the ability to defend an idea. We see it done every day with a variety of ideas and even products. There's the "apologetics" of abortion or its opposite, the Right to Life. There's conservatism versus liberalism or a market economy versus a planned economy (capitalism v. socialism or communism).

Apologetics is the give and take of ideas based on a person's knowledge, belief or understanding of those ideas. It's not only what you believe, but why you believe what you believe.

There are few things in life that are amazing to me. But God never ceases to amaze me. As I opened the Book of Acts, now purposefully and once again, the Holy Spirit grabbed hold of me and taught me. He allowed me to see that Acts is an absolute treasure trove of examples of Christian apologetics. Acts provides practical insights of how to speak to people about God and defend your Faith. Not only do you learn how, but you also learn what to do: the order of speech, the words to use. The Spirit highlights mentors we can imitate; Jesus was the "lead instructor" followed by Peter, Stephen, Barnabas, Paul and others.

Basically, the Book of Acts provides the three essentials of Christian Apologetics (or defending your Faith) that you need to learn: Structure, Definitions, and Strategies. And so, this study, *From Doubt to Defense* can be broken into the same three parts. Here's what we'll be examining...

Structure. The first weeks look at the overall "Structure" of Christian Apologetics. In other words, HOW to present your Apologetic or your defense of your Faith in Christ. Jesus Himself is the lead instructor to the disciples before He ascends to Heaven. Of course, the Holy Spirit immediately takes control and works through Peter and the remaining disciples. We'll also take a look at the issue of "speaking in tongues" (not necessarily what you may be thinking); there are some practical insights that are applicable for today.

Definitions. Over the next several weeks (if you're participating in a small group Bible study or Sunday school class) or as you traverse each chapter, we will examine the key definitions of apologetics – examining why we believe what we believe. We'll delve into our relationship to God: understanding who we are and whose we are, as well as the issues of sin and redemption. We'll also discuss what a person's worldview is, and how it can be influenced, changed or modified. Finally, we'll consider why it's crucial to understand the worldview of your audience when engaging in apologetics.

Unless and until we have a grasp of these issues, our personal apologetic will be weak and relatively ineffective. More than that, we will *feel* ineffective, and therefore insecure. However, if we have "prepped" ourselves by faith in His promise to the best of our ability, God is more than willing use our weakness to bring glory to Himself. In the end you will gain an understanding of the importance of Christian Theism, the foundation of our biblical faith.

Strategies. Finally, we put all of these Structure and Definition together with Strategies. The Apostle Paul was used brilliantly by God to bring His Gospel to the Roman world. Once a vehement unbeliever, God took Paul and used him, re-educating him to His purposes. And that's how we are to speak for God in our own days. We are to speak God's Truths powerfully, yet prayerfully, of God's Truths for the dual purpose of fearlessly defending God and His Word with the intent to bring others to Christ.

Today we battle against the new "heresies" (heresy is any belief or practice that directly and explicitly undermines the Gospel and its core teachings) of "open theism" and liberal theology as well as other popular philosophical "isms". The proper understanding of Romans 1:18 - 32 is absolutely critical when we "strategize" our personal apologetic.

Our world is facing many great crises. God has given all of His children - that means you and me - incredible opportunities to be witnesses to Who He is and what He desires in each and every person walking this earth. It is my sincere prayer that God will use this study to help you better understand your own Faith and embolden you to proclaim this liberating and life-saving message to the world around you.

Pray each day that God would use you in mighty and unbelievable ways, even today. I'll be keeping you in prayer as well. Let me know how God is using you.

Lesson 1 - Why Christian Theism?

Why do we have to be so particular? So why is CHRISTIAN Theism important?

So, we've been talking about the need to understand apologetics and the necessity of speaking God's Truth. We've looked at varying worldviews. But why do we need to be speaking of Christian theism? Why not "plain" theism?

First off, what is "theism"? Theism is the belief in God or god depending on your personal worldview. That's it. Plain and simple, not much better than deism. By contrast, deism is the idea that a god or some supernatural being created all that we see and all that there is. And then essentially, stepped back and out of the way. This type of god is impersonal or even non-personal. Theism is "better" in that it views God as the Creator but goes a step further in that God is "more personal" - as in can be "known" - and is interactive with his creation.

Before even starting a discussion of Christian apologetics, we have to lay a solid foundation of our knowledge and understanding of God. Without knowing (rudimentary) or understanding (rudimentary as well) Who God is, and who even Man is, we can't go on. We can state that God is the Creator, and we are the creature, but that's too simplistic. Man did not create God, He created us. The hierarchy of the entire universe, and our understanding of it, depends on God being at the very top with nothing else even coming close to Him in "being".

So, what is Christian Theism and why is it important?

Christian Theism is important because of God Himself. Every other religion or belief system has its followers chasing after or working towards "heaven" or "paradise" or some kind of "eternal life" in bliss and glory, believing that through our menial works alone, we can somehow and someday reach a point of "earning" that reward. We mistakenly believe that by occasionally giving to the poor, helping a widow or orphan, or even attempting to "solve" world poverty we can earn an eternal reward. The truth is no one can gain eternal life through their own good works or efforts. If salvation depended on our deeds, what hope would there be for those unable to perform such acts? Thankfully, our eternal reward is not based on what we do but on what Jesus has already done (Ephesians 2:8-9)

And that's where the whole idea of works completely implodes. You see, it's truly impossible to merit eternal life. And God understands that fact. It is impossible on our own, but the Christian idea of God does make it possible... under His terms.

Christian Theism is the idea of theism PLUS. Or maybe better said, fully realized through the true Biblical revelation of God. Christian Theism affirms that God exists in a Triune Nature of Father, Son and Holy Spirit. This is not three gods, but One God in Three Persons. After all is said and done, God has called us Christians to provide an apologetic or a defense for the God of the Bible, not just "some God."

Christian Theism incorporates the following ideas:
- God is "wholly other"; He is uncreated, eternal, omnipotent, immutable, etc.
- Human beings are completely limited with respect to fully understanding Him, His Being, His reasoning, and even the modalities of His goodness
- God in His goodness has created the physical world (universe) and from time to time directly intervenes in history for His purposes
- God is always Good and has good intentions for His creation (all of creation)
- God in His goodness has provided a way (the only way) to reconcile the fallen nature of the universe through the life, death, and resurrection of Jesus
- Accepting and receiving Jesus as your Savior is the only path to salvation

Before we continue, we must understand that some of our listeners (those we speak with) will argue with us about the veracity or importance of the Bible itself. "It's just a book of writings just like any other religion." Or "You can't trust the Bible... it's been translated too many times and has lost the original meaning." Or "There are so many contradictions in the Bible." Remember that many people that we interact with have probably never opened a Bible, never mind "studied" it. What many of our friends or family may respond with is what they have heard from various videos or podcasts or social media.

As believers, we trust the Bible because we have been taught it not only in church, but hopefully because we've been properly discipled by a more mature believer. As we daily open the pages of Scripture to explore, read, and study, we ought to be praying that the Holy Spirit illuminates in our minds and hearts what we are exploring, reading, and studying.

The Apostle Peter told us that we can trust the Bible and all of the teachings found throughout its pages. In 2 Peter 1:16-21, he writes, *"For we did not follow cleverly devised myths when we made known to you the power and coming of our Lord Jesus Christ, but we were eyewitnesses of his majesty. For when he received honor and glory from God the Father, and the voice was borne to him by the Majestic Glory, 'This is my beloved Son, with whom I am well pleased,' we ourselves heard this very voice borne from heaven, for we were with him on the holy mountain. And we have the prophetic word more fully confirmed, to which you will do well to pay attention as to a lamp shining in a dark place, until the day dawns and the morning star rises in your hearts, knowing this first of all, that no prophecy of Scripture comes from someone's own interpretation. For no prophecy was ever produced by the will of man, but men spoke from God as they were carried along by the Holy Spirit."*

American pastor, author, theologian, and educator Dr. Voddie Baucham provides this explanation as to why anyone should be able to trust the Bible, quoted from several of his sermons: *"I choose to believe the Bible because it is a reliable collection of historical documents* [written over a period of over 1,500 years by various authors in various locations, originally in three different languages (Hebrew, Greek, and Aramaic) of which there are over 6,000 complete or partial copies] *written down by eyewitnesses during the lifetime of other eyewitnesses* [especially the Gospels and the New Testament]; *they report to us supernatural events* [miracles in both Old and New Testaments] *that took place in fulfillment of specific prophecies* [both Old and New Testaments, no other religious writings have such information] *and claimed that their writings are divine rather than human* [writers of both Testaments make this claim] *in origin."*

The bottom line is that we can trust the Scriptures as well as its Author who is God Himself. But now the question is, Who is God?

We should not speak of God in vague, general terms as this diminishes His true nature. God is not the One on trial as we debate and reason with friends, loved ones and strangers - we are! It is our hearts, beliefs, and responses to His truth that are being tested.

If we truly believe that the Bible is the True, Inspired Word of God, spoken by God through ordinary men by the power of the Holy Spirit, then God is not on trial. The Bible does not merely assume the existence of God, the Bible *asserts* His eternal existence - "In the beginning, God created the heavens and the earth." Genesis 1:1. The Bible doesn't assume God; it *asserts* God. This existence is so important for us to grasp that without God, *nothing would or could exist*. He created everything, down to every last atom in the universe. And it was created *for* Him and no one else.

In and of itself that is a grand thought. And just as grand and just as marvelous is the knowledge that God Himself also created the perfect mechanism to redeem the creation that He knew would one day choose to disobey Him, thereby sinning, and fall out of fellowship. The supreme holiness of God demands that there would be complete separation between Himself and man. He knew that there was nothing man would be able to do about it. Man was completely and utterly helpless, but now because of Jesus Christ no longer hopeless.

The hope would lie in the Creator Himself. The Creator, in the image and person of Jesus Christ, would be the atoning sacrifice that would redeem sinful man, restoring eternal fellowship with Almighty God. The eternal destiny of every man, woman and child hinges on a crucial choice: to accept God's offer of salvation through Jesus or reject it. Those who place their faith in Christ as their personal Savior will experience the joy of eternal fellowship with Him in Heaven – a new world of perfect love, peace, and fulfillment. However, those who deny the redemption that the holy and sovereign God freely offers through Jesus will face the hell of eternal separation from Him. This isn't just a stark reality; it's a loving invitation. God's desire is that no one should perish, but that everyone would come to repentance and receive His gift of eternal life. The choice is real, and it matters deeply – but so does God's love, which is reaching out to every heart even now. God doesn't send people to hell; people choose hell themselves. Those are the only two choices. Period.

Some may say that we shouldn't argue with unbelievers. But that's not quite right. The Bible is very plain in that we are to reason or argue or discuss fully Who God is and what He has done for us - see Acts 17:2, 17, 18:4, 1 Peter 3:15, Acts 6:9, as examples. To simply say that God is love doesn't fully describe God. Our job is to know all of God and to reason with them. To show and demonstrate to them that God is the Sovereign, Creator of all that is. And that He wants to have a personal, permanent, and eternal relationship with His creation. We have that relationship on His terms, not ours.

The bottom line is this: are we sharing the Truth of God and the necessity of a personal and individual Salvation through the shed blood of Christ or the "feel good," or are we offering a watered-down, feel-good version of a "lovey-dovey" God who wouldn't dare send anyone to hell? Which one is the truth? The truth is that God's love is deep and real, but so is His holiness and justice. Salvation isn't about comforting words – it's about the life-saving message that Jesus died and rose again to rescue us from sin and eternal separation from God. Do we truly want our friends and loved ones with us in eternity in Heaven or not? This is serious eternal stuff. God's love is beyond measure, but He is not to be trifled with. That's why sharing the whole truth matters – not to condemn, but to offer the hope and salvation found only in Jesus.

Many say that Christianity is just one of the ways to get to God. It is just another religion. Jesus was just a "good man" or a wonderful prophet or an exemplary person to model your life after. Those facts are all true. But if Jesus isn't who He says He is and a simple man died on Calvary's cross rather than the Incarnate God, Christianity crumbles. Funny thing is that our Christian Faith stands the test of time. People still come to saving Faith in Christ and are forever changed. That is the power of the Gospel. That is the power in Christian Theism.

And so, before we dive into the meat of apologetics, we must ask three very foundational questions:

1. Who is God?
2. Who is Jesus?
3. Who is man and/or who am I?

Before continuing, take time to better know and understand Who God is, always has been, and always will be. Also take time to think about who you are. WRITE THESE NOTES OUT … and then towards the end of the study, compare or contrast what you've learned.

If we want to see as many people come to a saving faith in Christ, it is our duty to defend Christian Theism. And nothing less.

Lesson 1 – From Doubt to Defense – Defining Your World View – Three Fundamental Questions

Question One: Who is God? Part 1

Verses: Genesis 1:1, 26, Job 38, Mark 1:9-11

Key Questions:

What is the difference between "theism" and Christian theism?

Why is it important to understand the difference?

The Christian understanding of God: Christian Theism & the Tri-unity of God

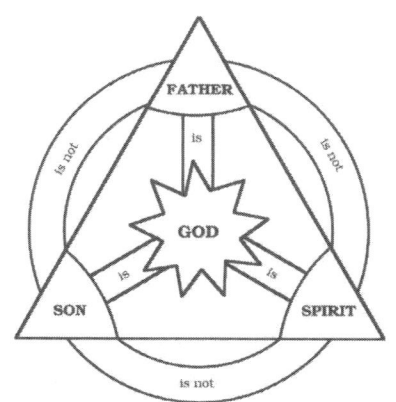

The members of the Holy Trinity are United, Distinct & Equal

"Trinity" is NOT mentioned in the Bible

The Trinity is NOT 3 gods

The Incommunicable "O's" & "I's" of God:

God's un- or not shared attributes. These attributes are not shared with any created being.

Omnipotent – all powerful;
don't buy into the straw man of God creating a rock He couldn't lift. That is a straw man argument – a deceptive tactic to take you off-point.

Omnipresent – all present; know the beginning from the end and the middle

Omniscient – all knowing; there is nothing that He does not know

Omnisapient – all wise; everything that He does is with perfect wisdom

Immutable – un or never changing; God doesn't "change" His mind

Independent – self-sustaining

Infinite – eternal; always was, is & will be

Indivisible – cannot be divided or broken down into parts; the members of the Trinity are of One Essence; the Trinity works as a whole

All of the above incommunicable attributes speak and contribute to God's…

Sovereignty – He is the absolute and only Ruler of the Universe whether seen or unseen, natural or supernatural. Everything was and is made for Him and for His honor and glory.

Copyright© Ronald Parrs 2024

Lesson 2 – Who is God...

and why this all matters...

Let me be completely upfront and honest, full disclosure: I am not a trained priest or pastor, teacher, theologian, Bible expositor, counselor, or anything else than what I do in my current profession. That said, I love learning, and the thing that I love learning most about is God and how He interacts with all of His creation. And, not to sound snobbish, but more specifically, how He interacts with me and how I am to interact with Him.

There are many excellent books that have already been written on this topic and there is no possible way that I can expound or add anything to any of them. The purpose of this chapter is to put forth several facts about God that I have gleaned in my personal study over the years. My hope is to present it in a relatively brief format so that it is coherent and understandable in regard to the topic of apologetics in general and to the general flow of this book in particular.

For brevity's sake, please take the time to search the Scriptures yourself by reading and studying the Bible. Then follow that up with reading through several of the resources mentioned at the end of this book.

Remember this: it is completely impossible to fully know and understand God. Our minds are not able to begin to grasp the immensity and enormity of Who He is and His involvement with His creation. He is Infinite; we are finite. God is Sovereign; we are subservient. He knows and understands everything; I can oftentimes figure out how to open a packaged meal or turn on my laptop. I have the ability to completely make a mess out of my life, while in His grace and mercy, He is all powerful to rescue me from my self-inflicted mess. In this life, if we are fortunate, He will provide us with brief glimpses of His power, His majesty, His provision, His love, His grace. Unfortunately for some, He will provide brief, yet impressive glimpses of His justice and possibly even His wrath.

In the last chapter, we ended by noting that there are three questions that must be answered before we can continue this conversation on apologetics and the importance of Christian theism. The questions are:

1. Who is God?
2. Who is Jesus?
3. Who is man and/or who am I?

First, who is God? That is the question of the ages for many people. I'm going to forgo that philosophical discussion and launch right into what the Bible says about Him from Genesis to Revelation. By no means is this comprehensive, but we have to have a foundation.

As we've already stated, God is Triune in nature. There exists One God in Three Persons, Father, Son, and Holy Spirit. These three Persons are of one essence. Essence is what makes a thing what it is. In basic terms, there are three essential parts to His essence:

1. God is Eternal – He has always existed. He had no beginning and will have no end. God has never not existed.

2. God is Essential – In order for anything to exist, God must exist. He created it (every physical and metaphysical thing) as well as every law (scientific and mathematic) to continue that existence.

3. God is Equal – the Persons of the God-head, Father, Son, and Holy Spirit are equally eternal, essential, omniscient, omnipotent, omnisapient (all wise), omnipresent, self-sufficient (asciety, God needs nothing else), immutable (unchanging) all of the time.

God has attributes. Those listed above are some of His "incommunicable" attributes. Those attributes are His alone. If He were to share them, He would cease to be God.

In the Persons of the God-head we have three distinct "roles" or "functions"; they are not "hierarchies" because they are equally God. Certain of the roles are shared, others are distinct.

The Father's role is the One who "chooses" (see Ephesians 1:3-14). He is the Creator and Ruler of the universe (Genesis 1:1, Matthew 11:25). The Father is He who "sends forth" that which is needed to do His will, whether it be the other Members of the God-head or angels or plagues.

The Son's role is the One who directly represents and reflects the God-head to mankind. For a brief time, ordinary men and women were able to eat, drink, walk with, converse, touch, and physically be with the Son. The Son was also integral in Creation itself (the Word; Genesis 1:1, John 1:3). In His role as the Word, He preserves and sustains all things (Hebrew 1:3, Colossians 1:17). In the future, the Son will be the Judge of all things (John 5:22, 8:16).

The role of the Holy Spirit is quite remarkable in so many ways. The Holy Spirit: instructs (Nehemiah 9:20, John 14:2, 6), Speaks (Mark 13:11, Acts 13:2), Intercedes (Romans 8:26), Gives spiritual life (John 6:63), Inspires Scripture (2 Tim 3:16), Convicts men and women of their sin (John 16:7-8), and he also Indwells believers (John 14:17, Romans 8:9, 1 Corinthians 6:19).

In short, God the Father creates the plan, God the Son invokes the plan, and God the Holy Spirit reveals the plan

These are the things that make God unique and essential for everything.

Returning the idea of attributes, God has also chosen to "communicate" certain of His attributes to His creation, man, for the purpose of relationship but also to reflect back Who He is to the rest of creation. At best, we humans created in the image and likeness of God, do a mediocre if not imperfect job of using or demonstrating these attributes. Some of these attributes, we demonstrate terribly. For example, we know how to love, show mercy or grace or holiness; we are able to judge, create, and forgive; we are able to demonstrate wrath, as well as wisdom and truth.

Let's end the list there. I think you get the point. God is supremely larger and more grand than we can possibly comprehend or grasp. That's what makes Him God.

Second, who is Jesus? Jesus is the Son, a direct reflection of the Father, sent by the Father to do the will of the Father in redeeming and restoring mankind back into relationship with God. Jesus is the second member of the God-head, co-equal with the Father and the Holy Spirit. Jesus is eternal. Jesus is the Word of God made flesh who dwelt among man for a season.

Jesus was fully human and fully God at the same time. As Deity, Jesus chose to put aside His eternality for that season in order to fulfill the plan and will of the Father.

In Divinity, Jesus sustained nature (calmed the sea, caused a tree to whither); nature had to obey Him. Jesus had the ability to provide enough meals for thousands of people with almost no supplies. Because He had compassion for His creation, Jesus healed the sick, gave sight to the blind, and even brought the dead back to life.

Being fully human, Jesus is able to completely understand us in every way. Jesus was conceived in a completely different way, but then gestated like every human has since Adam's first offspring. He passed through the birth canal and grew as a child under the supervision of earthly parents. From time to time, Jesus caused His parents certain amounts of angst. He went through puberty and then matured into adulthood. He understands our temptations, our frustrations, our pain, our grief, our sorrow, our joy. As a man, He played, and He worked; He laughed and He cried; He hugged those closest to Him in life and then He spread His arms wide to redeem us in His sacrificial atoning death on the cross.

As God, Jesus proved His Deity by raising Himself from the dead by the will of the Father and then ascended into Heaven where He is preparing a place for all those who believe in His finished work and accept Him as their one and only Lord and Savior. One day soon, He will come to gather His people to Himself and eventually and forever completely do away with evil, sin, and death.

The first time Jesus dwelt among His creation, He came humbly and quietly. He arrived with barely anyone noticing. When He returns to take back what is rightfully His, Jesus will come with majesty and power. Upon His return, every living thing on this planet, even all creation, will witness Him as He is in majesty and power, the Lord Almighty, Creator of Heaven and earth.

That, my friends, is my Jesus!

Last of all, who is man? Who am I?

Let's start by saying that I know that I'm a human being. I was born in the mid-twentieth century in the United States of America. I, like every one of you, came into this world completely needy, not being able to provide anything for my sustenance nor well-being. I was, and to a certain degree even now, am completely dependent on … everyone for almost everything. I, like you, entered the world completely empty-handed and will leave this world, completely empty-handed.

I have had absolutely no control over who my parents were, nor my ethnicity nor gender. I had no control over the timing of my birth. I have had little control over how my life has progressed (maybe regressed?).

After my wife passed into glory and I closed my business after forty plus years, God forced me to ask the question: Who am I Lord? And then after that question, what do you want of me Lord, who do You want me to be?

In God's economy, it is more important who I am being rather than what I am doing. Being a child of God and having a proper relationship with Him is infinitely more important than what I am doing. God is the One Who gives me life and therefore a purpose for now in this temporal life and for eternity.

Lesson 2 – From Doubt to Defense – Three Fundamental Questions

Question One: Who is God?

The Trinity

There exists ONE God in 3 Persons

The "God-head" consists of:

1. Essence –

   Eternal –

   Essential –

   Equal –

2. Person – the "Roles" or "Functions" of the Persons of the Deity are

   God the Father _____

   God the Son _____

   God the Holy Spirit _____

What distinguishes God from everything else in all of Creation? Some of God's attributes are "communicable" (transferable to man) others are incommunicable".

God the Father

Attributes

Roles or Actions

God the Son

Attributes

Roles or Actions

God the Holy Spirit

Attributes

Roles or Actions

Similarities:

Differences:

Question Two: Who is Jesus?

Verses: Luke 1:31, 3:21-38, Philippians 2:6-11, Hebrews 1:1-12

Key Questions:
Why is understanding & knowing that Jesus is fully human important?
Why does this matter?

Proofs of Jesus humanity:

Birth or Incarnation

Life & Ministry

Suffering & Death

Question Two: Who is Jesus? ... continued

Verses: Philippians 2:5-11, Psalm 22, 110, Isaiah 53, John 11, Matthew 28

Key Questions:
Why is understanding & knowing that Jesus is fully God important?
Why does this matter?

Proofs of Jesus Divinity:

Birth or Incarnation

Life & Ministry

Suffering & Death

Question Three: Who is Man? (Who am I?)

Verses: Genesis 1:26-28, 2:15-25; Psalm 8

Key Questions:
What makes us human beings?
Why does this matter?

Answering the key questions above:

1. Who am I?

2. Where did I come from?

3. Where am I going?

4. What is my purpose?

5. What about morality & ethics?

6. Understanding us helps us better understand God & vice versa.

Homework: Think about your understanding of what it means to have "dominion over the earth"

Copyright© Ronald Parrs 2025

Lesson 3 - Getting Started Requires a Good Start

Now that we're well into the 21st century, God has gifted us Christians with incredible opportunities to share the Gospel of Jesus Christ.

The world around us is confused. I would go so far as to say even frightened, as Islam intrudes western society, liberals (progressives) attempt a "remake" of traditional American society and our moral as well as cultural infrastructure crumbles.

1 Peter 3:15 - 16, admonishes us to have an answer for the hope that we demonstrate to the world. And when we present an answer, we are to do it with love and respect.

"...but in your hearts honor Christ the Lord as holy, always being prepared to make a defense to anyone who asks you for a reason for the hope that is in you; yet do it with gentleness and respect, having a good conscience, so that, when you are slandered, those who revile your good behavior in Christ may be put to shame."

2 Peter 3:14 - 18 is a bit stronger describing the urgency and complexity of WHY we will need to be strong in our convictions.

Here's the text: *"Therefore, beloved, since you are waiting for these, be diligent to be found by him without spot or blemish, and at peace. And count the patience of our Lord as salvation, just as our beloved brother Paul also wrote to you according to the wisdom given him, as he does in all his letters when he speaks in them of these matters. There are some things in them that are hard to understand, which the ignorant and unstable twist to their own destruction, as they do the other Scriptures. You therefore, beloved, knowing this beforehand, take care that you are not carried away with the error of lawless people and lose your own stability. But grow in the grace and knowledge of our Lord and Savior Jesus Christ. To Him be the glory both now and to the day of eternity. Amen."*

We too are to be bold in our witness as the apostle Paul not only teaches, but we must also show the *type* of boldness that we see throughout the book of Acts (9:28, 13:46, 18:26 for example). You see, the world isn't looking for "wishy-washy" "make me feel good" teaching (it may say that, but that's not the truth). The world around us - our neighbors, family, co-workers, classmates and, dare I say even enemies and strangers - are really ready for truth and conviction. They want something they can grab and hold onto. They're looking for a reason to live.

The Book of the Acts of the Apostles, written by Evangelist Luke – a first century CE physician of Greek heritage and devoted evangelist – shows through both words and actions how to effectively handle apologetics. It is a powerful example to learn how to present a clear, compelling defense of the Gospel, making it an essential guide for anyone seeking to share their faith with confidence and truth.

Christian brothers and sisters, we have NOTHING to be ashamed of, nothing to apologize for. God goes before us to strengthen and protect us; to provide us wisdom and power. In Romans 1:16, Paul states, *"For I am not ashamed of the gospel, for it is the power of God for salvation to everyone who believes, to the Jew first and also to the Greek."*

Context matters

Before we continue, we must look back at what Peter first told the church, because having a proper understanding of who we are (I am) and what our (my) attitude ought to be is the difference between winning an argument for argument's sake and winning souls (making disciples) for eternity.

Peter knew who he was: a nobody who eventually became a somebody because he met, knew, and was discipled by the One Body that truly matters. We need to have a firm yet humble grasp on who we were and are, and how Jesus transformed us, before we can think of being God's tools that will allow us to participate in Peter's admonitions of the above two passages. The earlier chapters of 1 Peter speak to these issues.

So, according to Peter, who are we? We are strangers (exiles) and sojourners in a foreign land, waging war against our own minds and bodies (1 Peter 2:11). When we came to Jesus, what did we become? We became chosen and holy, a royal priesthood (1 Peter 2:9). Why was all of this change necessary? This was necessary so that through the Holy Spirit, we would be used to proclaim God's excellencies, demonstrating mercy and grace through right and holy living, surrounded by a world that may even hate us. (1 Peter 2:9-12).

And what of our (my) attitude and how we should live? Both Peter and later Paul would write directly about our attitude. Be subject to one another. Wives to husbands, with husbands sacrificially loving their wives. Children being obedient to their parents. Employees are subject to their supervisors and employers. Citizens being mindful of their government, which is ordained by God. Review these passages: 1 Peter 3:1-7, Ephesians 6:1, 1 Peter 2:13-24. Furthermore, we are as Christian to be in unity with one another, to demonstrate sympathy and love, having a tender heart and humble mind. Followers of Jesus Christ are called to be blessings not, curses (1 Peter 3:8-9).

Why do we do all this? Because it's exactly what Jesus did (Philippians 2:1-11). Jesus temporarily put aside divinity and took on mortality so that He could sinlessly serve His creation – us. Recall what Jesus did in the Garden as He was being arrested: Jesus could have called down twelve legions of angels to "save" Himself from these enemies. Instead, He understood His mission and the Father's plan that needed to be fulfilled. Jesus took on the full "wrath" of men because He was about to take on and experience the full Wrath of Almighty God, which was death and separation. Are we (am I) willing to go that far for my family, friends, and, I daresay, "enemies"?

In debate or apologetics, if I've won the argument but haven't won the soul or even be heard again, I've lost the entire exercise… and God is not glorified.

The Basics of Christian Apologetics: 3 Steps

But how do we do that? Many think that just because we're not Bible scholars or pastors or Sunday school teachers, we aren't capable of presenting a good defense of Christ. Trust me, I thought the same way and I believed a lie from the pit of hell itself. Over the past several years God has been teaching me how to salt and pepper everyday conversations with His truth.

Let's look at the Book of Acts and learn. In the very first paragraphs of Chapter one, Jesus Christ Himself demonstrates what we are to do and how we are to be His witnesses.

Verses 2 through 5 read: *"until the day when he was taken up, after he had given commands through the Holy Spirit to the apostles whom he had chosen. He presented himself alive to them after his suffering by many proofs, appearing to them during forty days and speaking about the kingdom of God.*

And while staying with them he ordered them not to depart from Jerusalem, but to wait for the promise of the Father, which, he said, 'you heard from me; for John baptized with water, but you will be baptized with the Holy Spirit not many days from now.'"

In verse 2 we learn that it's the Holy Spirit who teaches us. Our responsibility is to daily crack open the Bible, read, and then pray about what we've read. The Holy Spirit, the third person of the Godhead, God, teaches us what we are to know. Furthermore, He provides us with the wisdom with which to use this knowledge. To be brutally honest, up until recently, daily Bible reading, never mind study, was difficult for me and I would make excuses. Finally I'm beginning to come to the point where I can't participate in the day without being in God's Word; even if it's for ten minutes. It is nourishment for my heart, soul and life.

God's Word is so powerful, yet we neglect to bring it into our lives, to the point of it taking over our thought process. We are to, as the apostle Paul in admonishes 2 Corinthians 10:5, "take every thought captive." God's Word, dwelling in our minds and hearts will gradually and sufficiently transform us to the image of Christ.

But back to Acts. Allowing the Holy Spirit to teach us is step one. We have to make that conscious effort to let God's Word speak to us in order to teach us His ways. In verses 3 through 5, Jesus Himself demonstrates HOW we are to serve as His witnesses and to give an apologetic for His Gospel.

Verse 3 is the start. Notice that Jesus provided the disciples many convincing proofs of His bodily Resurrection. Jesus "showed Himself," He ***appeared*** to them over a course of 40 days. In other words, Jesus demonstrates that before any apology or defense can be made, we have to appear. We have to "show up." Oftentimes, that's the problem. We don't show up. We avoid situations or relationships that God has placed us in for the purpose of sharing His Good News. That's an incredible privilege that He has given us! Think about it, if we just showed up half the time, people around us might actually "see" us doing a "good work" or even opening our mouths for the Glory of God.

When we "show up," it is also necessary for us to "stand up"; we can't just show up and then sit on the sidelines as a barely interested listener. Let's be honest, it's often hard to stand up for truth and what is right, especially when we're alone and possibly outnumbered. As soon as we stand, others can plainly see us, and some may even recognize us. But when we stand up, we are likely empowering others to stand up as well. As we stand shoulder to shoulder, we demonstrate not only our commitment, but our unity – in thought and in action.

Which leads us to the next step. In that same verse, we see that Jesus directly *spoke* to His disciples about God and the Kingdom of Heaven. So yes, we are to show up, and then (not but) we are to speak. I think many of us don't truly realize how powerful the spoken word is. From a divine perspective, God chose to use the spoken word created the heavens and the earth. He created everything by simply speaking (except Man - Man, God created by forming him from the dust of the earth, mankind is a special creation because we are God's image bearers - another discussion). Also, by speaking, He will take it away and bring forth a new creation in its appointed time.

God has provided the human race with this incredible attribute of speech and a spoken language using knowledge and wisdom. No other living creature on the planet has those combined abilities. God doesn't want us wasting our time speaking of trifling matters, He wants us speaking of Him; reflecting back to God His Glory. To tell the world (our friends, family and neighbors and strangers) what God has done and is doing in our lives. The mere fact that God chose you as one of His very own is an awesome thing. Why don't or won't we share that?

Finally, from time to time, we are to offer a "*command*." I understand that as actually quoting Scripture or at least providing a solid Biblical truth. Now don't start telling me that you can never memorize Scripture. That's just not true. Think about how many songs you've "memorized" just listening to an album or the radio or your favorite electronic device. Surely learning God's Word is much more important than a Top 40 "hit" to your life.

When we are in the Bible on a really regular basis (like every day), we just aren't getting into the Bible, the Bible is getting into US! That's the Holy Spirit working. In the beginning, we start recognizing or remembering verses, "oh yeah, that's..." or we fumble "I think I read in ..." And that's a great start. Have you ever noticed that the more you read God's Word, the better you know it? And by the same token, God's Word begins to "know" you and speaks to you in various ways. God's Word is not only powerful, but also personal.

So that's how we start our personal defense of God and His Word. We *show up* to the world around us. We *speak* about what God has and is doing in our lives. We lovingly and correctly quote His Word, being sure to not take or use verses out of context; we *command*. *"For the word of God is living and active, sharper than any two-edged sword, piercing to the division of soul and of spirit, of joints and of marrow, and discerning the thoughts and intentions of the heart."* Hebrews 4:12.

Why did about 3,000 people who witnessed this repent and turn back to God, seeking forgiveness, and then were baptized to demonstrate their faith publicly? All of this was accomplished because Peter showed up, stood up, spoke up, shared God's Truths, which reminded the crowd that each and every one of them had a direct responsibility in Jesus's trial and death just weeks earlier. Peter, like Jesus, wasn't afraid to remind people of their sin and their commitment to God. When we allow the Holy Spirit to move us to action, as He did with Peter, there's no limit to what can be done in furthering God's Kingdom.

Now go and be used of God for His good works and for His Glory. Remember, it's not about you. It IS about Him.

Lesson 3 – From Doubt to Defense – Getting Started Requires a Good Start

Verses: 1 Peter 3:15 – 16, 2 Peter 3:15 – 18 & Acts 1:1 - 11

Key Questions:

What is the study of Apologetics and why is it necessary?

What & How does God teach us about apologetics?

Apologetics: the presentation of a good defense of an idea or cause or doctrine

Why discuss Apologetics? 1 Peter 3:15 – 16, 2 Peter 3:15 – 18

The Basics of Apologetics: Acts 1:1 – 11

The entire Godhead teaches us: Father, Son & Holy Spirit.

The work of the Holy Spirit: verse 2

The work of the Son: verses 3 – 5. How & what does Jesus do to instruct us in the work of Apologetics?

    1. Verse 3 – Show up; take advantage of situations

    2. Verse 3 – Speak; be willing to open your mouth. God will speak for you when necessary

    3. Verse 4 – Command or share scripture or a Biblical truth. People are looking for absolutes

    This means that you have to be in God's Word on a daily basis.

The work of the Father: the entire passage. The Father is behind every aspect.

Copyright© Ronald Parrs 2025

Lesson 4 - Speaking in Tongues

Looking to start an argument? Let's talk about "speaking in tongues." Yeah, that will get some discussion going!

Christians can sometimes look foolish by how we behave toward others. But to the unbeliever, this can look more like a side-show. The Gospel is tarnished and mocked.

Did "speaking in tongues" happen? Of course! Just take a look at Acts Chapter 2, verse 4. *"And they were all filled with the Holy Spirit and began to speak in other tongues as the Spirit gave them utterance."*

The question is, what are "other tongues?" Frankly, I'm not going to dive into all the theological details right now. What really matters is asking: what gospel truth should drive us in this situation?

But what I do think is important is the *idea* of "speaking in tongues" as it applies to HOW we speak or talk to other people. Anyone who is married or has children must speak to the spouse and children in different ways and words. If you're in some type of leadership position, we must understand the people we lead and how they best learn. For those who teach and instruct, do we understand how the student listens, understands, and finally grasps and applies those principles and skills. We men must put in and turn on our "feminine hearing aid" or put on our "feminine glasses" in order to "listen" to our wives or understand how they may see a certain issue. In other words, we "hear the words" but we don't understand the "hidden" meaning behind them. The same is true for women listening to and understanding men.

What are "Tongues"?

Words are just words, and we have to understand what they mean. What they mean in their context. What they mean personally. The adage that a "picture speaks a thousand words" is very true and we need to learn something from that. If you have ever traveled outside of your native country or sometimes locality, you know that when you hear a conversation going on in your native tongue or accent, you are naturally drawn to it; it is familiar; it is comfortable and comforting.

Here's the text of Acts 2:1 - 12:

"When the day of Pentecost arrived, they were all together in one place. And suddenly there came from heaven a sound like a mighty rushing wind, and it filled the entire house where they were sitting. And divided tongues as of fire appeared to them and rested on each one of them. And they were all filled with the Holy Spirit and began to speak in other tongues as the Spirit gave them utterance.

"Now there were dwelling in Jerusalem Jews, devout men from every nation under heaven. And at this sound the multitude came together, and they were bewildered, because each one was hearing them speak in his own language. And they were amazed and astonished, saying, 'Are not all these who are speaking Galileans? And how is it that we hear, each of us in his own native language? Parthians and Medes and Elamites and residents of Mesopotamia, Judea and Cappadocia, Pontus and Asia, Phrygia and Pamphylia, Egypt and the parts of Libya belonging to Cyrene, and visitors from Rome, both Jews and proselytes, Cretans and Arabians—we hear them telling in our own tongues the mighty works of God.' And all were amazed and perplexed, saying to one another, 'What does this mean?'"

The background context of Acts 2 is the city of Jerusalem, a relatively cosmopolitan zone - although considered "backwater" - in the Roman Empire during a feast time where many people from all over the known world were gathered for not only commerce, but to celebrate the Jewish Passover and time of Pentecost, big holidays in those times. And these folks would be there for an extended time simply because it took a lot of time just to get there or anywhere for that matter. There were Parthians and Medes (from the area of modern-day Turkey and Iran), Egyptians, Libyans, and others. Each had his or her own culture as well as language. And on that particular day that God ordained, something astonishing happened that grabbed their attention. It wasn't coincidence that these people from far-flung parts of the Roman Empire were in Jerusalem. God had a purpose and a plan for their lives.

On that special day they heard in their own, respective language and dialect, "the wonders of God." Now mind you, many of these people were no doubt polytheists; they believed in multiple gods. A single God as the Jews believed was somewhat "novel" or even "Jewish". They had heard of monotheistic teachings, but it wasn't the norm. And now, going beyond plain monotheism, something completely mind-blowing was about to invade their thoughts: there exists a PERSONAL and TRI-UNE God. A God who was (is) willing to condescend to His creation and offer true and everlasting fellowship.

Works were about to be exploded (actually already had been in the finished work of Jesus at the Cross and His resurrection 3 days later) and "simple" belief and humble faith was and forever would be the paradigm shift to commune with your God. No more bloody sacrifices or worthless chanting and rituals. Don't underestimate the significance of that shift - even in today's context. We come to God through Christ by Faith alone, not by our personal "good" works.

Know your audience

When it comes to speaking to and with others about the Bible, Christianity, and sharing our faith, we must understand our audience. We see another example of this in Acts chapter 17, where the apostle Paul is in Athens, waiting for his ministry companions Silas and Timothy. Paul proceeded as he typically would, seeking out the local Jewish population by speaking in the various synagogues, and then proceeded to the local marketplace. We read:

16 Now while Paul was waiting for them at Athens, his spirit was provoked within him as he saw that the city was full of idols. 17 So he reasoned in the synagogue with the Jews and the devout persons, and in the marketplace every day with those who happened to be there. 18 Some of the Epicurean and Stoic philosophers also conversed with him. And some said, "What does this babbler wish to say?" Others said, "He seems to be a preacher of foreign divinities"—because he was preaching Jesus and the resurrection. 19 And they took him and brought him to the Areopagus, saying, "May we know what this new teaching is that you are presenting? 20 For you bring some strange things to our ears. We wish to know therefore what these things mean." ²¹ Now all the Athenians and the foreigners who lived there would spend their time in nothing except telling or hearing something new.

²² So Paul, standing in the midst of the Areopagus, said: "Men of Athens, I perceive that in every way you are very religious. ²³ For as I passed along and observed the objects of your worship, I found also an altar with this inscription: 'To the unknown god.' What therefore you worship as unknown, this I proclaim to you. ²⁴ The God who made the world and everything in it, being Lord of heaven and earth, does not live in temples made by man, ²⁵ nor is he served by human hands, as though he needed anything, since he himself gives to all mankind life and breath and everything. ²⁶ And he made from one man every nation of mankind to live on all the face of the earth, having determined allotted periods and the boundaries of their dwelling place, ²⁷ that they should seek God, and perhaps feel their way toward him and find him. Yet he is actually not far from each one of us, ²⁸ for

"'In him we live and move and have our being'; as even some of your own poets have said, "'For we are indeed his offspring.'

²⁹ Being then God's offspring, we ought not to think that the divine being is like gold or silver or stone, an image formed by the art and imagination of man. ³⁰ The times of ignorance God overlooked, but now he commands all people everywhere to repent, ³¹ because he has fixed a day on which he will judge the world in righteousness by a man whom he has appointed; and of this he has given assurance to all by raising him from the dead."

³² Now when they heard of the resurrection of the dead, some mocked. But others said, "We will hear you again about this." ³³ So Paul went out from their midst. ³⁴ But some men joined him and believed, among whom also were Dionysius the Areopagite and a woman named Damaris and others with them.

We read in this passage that Paul was no longer speaking with the "common" people; instead, the Holy Spirit had prompted him to talk with the learned or educated men and leaders of the city. They were not only leaders but also philosophers and students of the Epicurean and Stoic schools of philosophy. Paul needed to approach and speak with them in a different language.

In the synagogues, Paul could refer back to the Law and Tanach. Amongst these learned gentiles, he referenced their "unknown" God, revealing the truths of the Creator of the Universe. Although we can argue that Paul was highly educated, it was the Holy Spirit who provided him with the knowledge and the words he needed. Each of us needs to address the same dependency when speaking to our particular audience.

In chapter 11, "The Unbeliever's Worldview", we'll delve deeper into this passage. For now, though, before opening our mouths to speak, we must know our audience and their needs, then pray, asking the Holy Spirit for the correct words, how to best communicate God's truths with them while demonstrating the right attitude.

Practical Tongues

Now for the practical application. How do we speak to our co-worker about Jesus? How about your Jewish classmate? How about the guy behind the convenience store counter whose nametag reads "Mohammed"? How about that blatantly atheistic, "in your face" Political Science or Philosophy professor in college? What about the homeless person that we see when we give our time in the local soup kitchen? How about the other moms and dads on our kids' sports teams? Are we speaking to them about the "wonders of God" in a tongue that they will understand? Have we allowed the Holy Spirit to come upon us Christians in order to take control of our minds and thoughts and give Glory to God for what He has personally done in our lives? Have we – have I – taken the time to be in God's Word and to pray about who to talk to?

God has given all of us Christians a truly unbelievable time in world history to carry out the Great Commission. The opportunities abound. We live in a lost and decaying and dying world that, believe it or not, is hungering and thirsting for righteousness and godliness (perhaps under the guise of so-called "fairness").

One of the greatest things about being a truly born-again believer in Jesus Christ is that we have a personal story of how we came to a saving knowledge and relationship with Him. Each story is individual. Each story is personal. Each story is relevant. No one can deny our personal experience of how the Lord God Almighty chose to intervene in our personal lives to save our individual souls.

Maybe your story feels pretty ordinary – you grew up going to church and lived a normal life – but deep down, you knew that something was missing until you met Jesus. Your story may be extraordinary as God chose to save you from alcoholism or drug abuse or prostitution and when you finally hit bottom, looked up and cried out to God for salvation, He was there… waiting like the prodigal Father, welcoming you home. Either way, ordinary or extraordinary, it's your story of how God restored and redeemed you and your life for eternity.

Here's the final question for both you and me: Does the way we talk about God make men, women, and children pause, think deeper, and wonder, "What does this mean?" Does it stir something in them, pushing them beyond what they already know about God and Christianity. That, my friend, is *your* "welcome" into conversation(s) that could change *their* lives for eternity. They want *us* to help them answer that question. That's how we begin to apply 1 Peter 3:15. We must learn what their language is and how to best speak it for the purpose of sharing the Truths of God.

That's what I believe "speaking in tongues" is really all about: introducing people to Jesus Christ.

A final question: What language do I need to speak to the new or younger generations for them to be saved?

Jesus' message to them is the same: His life, His purpose on earth, His death and resurrection, but… what methods should we use to reach them?

Lesson 4 – From Doubt to Defense – Speaking in Tongues

Verses: Acts 2:1 – 12

Key Questions:
What is the work of the Holy Spirit in our lives?
Are we speaking in "tongues" that our society can hear & understand?

Tongues: the presentation of the Gospel of Jesus Christ using words that the hearer will hear, listen to and understand

What do we have to do to allow the Holy Spirit to work in our lives? Acts 2:1 – 4

What are "other tongues" in today's society? Acts 2: 6 – 11

Home

School

Workplace

Grocery store

House party

What other examples can you think of when you need to speak in "another tongue"?

What are we speaking about when we talk to people in the world around us? Acts 2:11

Copyright© Ronald Parrs 2025

Spiritual Gifts

All of us are in search of significance and relevance.

For us Christians, we must - and I would probably go so far as to say we are required - to break and even destroy that worldly definition. We have to understand Whose we are.

The apostle Paul writing to the Corinthian church put it this way:

"Or do you not know that your body is a temple of the Holy Spirit within you, whom you have from God? You are not your own, for you were bought with a price. So glorify God in your body." 1 Corinthians 6:19-20.

Sadly, the context of the verse above deals with immorality (*porneia*) in all its destructive ways, including joining with a prostitute, whether literally or figuratively. But when you think about it, as we look for significance from the world, we are in many ways, prostituting ourselves. Instead of drawing close to the One Who truly loves us for who we are, we draw close to those people and things that only choose to use us for temporary gain.

In the book of Acts chapters two through eight, we read about and see several people who initially drew their significance and relevance from the world. They were ordinary men and women who had and sought significance from their peers. In a way, they wanted their plan for life to be God's Plan, rather than -initially anyway - adopting God's Plan for their life. Once they accepted Jesus as their personal Lord and Savior and let the Holy Spirit come into their respective lives, God's Gifts were bestowed on them and the world was turned upside down forever!

I don't know about you, but that's real significance and relevance. They became significant in God's eyes first.

Let's look at three of these men and their Spiritual Gifts.

In Acts chapter two, we find Simon, otherwise known as Peter. To his family and friends, he was a Galilean fisherman, a relative nobody. His "world" would have preferred to keep him in his place. Being a fisherman was lowly enough but being a Galilean was a step below. Being from Galilee was almost as bad as being from Samaria, although you were still considered a Jew; a "hick" maybe but a Jew nonetheless.

So what did God do with *Simon bar Jonah* (meaning "son of Jonah") whom Jesus would take and remake into *Cephas* or *Peter*? You may find it helpful to know that Cephas means "rock" in the Aramaic dialect of Hebrew. *Petros* means "rock" in Greek. Peter was the little rock. Jesus is *the* Rock. For three years Jesus would work with him and mold him, but it wasn't until Jesus was taken back to Heaven that Peter would finally receive the gifts that God had intended him to have. The people were astonished to hear the disciples (who would become apostles) speak in tongues (their respective languages), but now they would witness a common fisherman deliver a speech or sermon that would not only inspire, but would cause people to ask, "what shall we do [to be saved]."

Peter, though an ordinary man, was filled with the knowledge and wisdom of God's Word. He not only quoted King David from the Psalms but also referenced the minor prophet Joel – an often-overlooked book among Christians. Despite its relative obscurity, the Holy Spirit brought Joel's prophecy to Peter's mind, enabling him to interpret and apply it correctly. This demonstrates how God equips His servants (even you and me) with understanding, even of less familiar Scriptures, to proclaim His truth effectively.

"But this is what was uttered through the prophet Joel:

"'And in the last days it shall be, God declares,
that I will pour out my Spirit on all flesh,
and your sons and your daughters shall prophesy,
   and your young men shall see visions,
   and your old men shall dream dreams;
even on my male servants and female servants
   in those days I will pour out my Spirit, and they shall prophesy.
And I will show wonders in the heavens above
   and signs on the earth below,

blood, and fire, and vapor of smoke;
the sun shall be turned to darkness
   and the moon to blood,
   before the day of the Lord comes, the great and magnificent day.
And it shall come to pass that everyone who calls upon the name of the Lord shall be saved.'" Acts 2:16-21 quoting Joel 2:28-32.

Peter was also gifted with preaching and prophecy. In chapter 3 we read of his being given the gift of physical healing. In time, he would soon be gifted with being an apostle. Peter would shed his worldly "significance" and take on God's idea of significance, taking God's Word and God's Gospel of Hope and Salvation into the Jewish community and beyond. A simple man became one of a handful that God would use to change the world in order to reconcile it to Himself. That is true significance.

Later in life, Peter would write to fellow believers and tell them about the Spiritual Gifts that God willingly bestows on His children (1 Peter 4).

Not only were the apostles blessed with Spiritual Gifts, but others as well.

In chapters two, three, four and six, the Holy Spirit provides Gifts to the Church at large. Most notably, we see gifts of service, encouragement, leadership (administration), generosity and hospitality. The believers helped to take care of one another. They shared their possessions.

When it came to figuring out how best to take care of people's needs, the apostles set aside deacons to do the labor of tending to physical needs thereby allowing them to study and preach God's Word. Leaders can't do everything! Our pastors can't do everything. We read in Acts chapter 6:

"Now in these days when the disciples were increasing in number, a complaint by the Hellenists arose against the Hebrews because their widows were being neglected in the daily distribution. And the twelve summoned the full number of the disciples and said, 'It is not right that we should give up preaching the word of God to serve tables. Therefore, brothers, pick out from among you seven men of good repute, full of the Spirit and of wisdom, whom we will

appoint to this duty. But we will devote ourselves to prayer and to the ministry of the word.' And what they said pleased the whole gathering, and they chose Stephen, a man full of faith and of the Holy Spirit, and Philip, and Prochorus, and Nicanor, and Timon, and Parmenas, and Nicolaus, a proselyte of Antioch. These they set before the apostles, and they prayed and laid their hands on them.

"And the word of God continued to increase, and the number of the disciples multiplied greatly in Jerusalem, and a great many of the priests became obedient to the faith." Acts 6:1-7

We believers must come alongside our pastors and teachers to further minister to the general flock. Praying for our pastors and leaders is good, but when God endows you with gifts and talents, then use them! We are called to do as well as to be. That's why God, by the power of the Holy Spirit, has gifted all believers with certain gifts. We aren't to hog or hoard our gifts for our personal use and profit. Instead, we are to use them for God's purposes and His glory.

Stephen, as noted with the deacons above became a great, gift laden man of the Spirit. We don't know too much about him, but what he did was significant in God's eyes and was used in a special way. In Acts 6 we read:

"And Stephen, full of grace and power, was doing great wonders and signs among the people. Then some of those who belonged to the synagogue of the Freedmen (as it was called), and of the Cyrenians, and of the Alexandrians, and of those from Cilicia and Asia, rose up and disputed with Stephen. But they could not withstand the wisdom and the Spirit with which he was speaking. Then they secretly instigated men who said, 'We have heard him speak blasphemous words against Moses and God.' And they stirred up the people and the elders and the scribes, and they came upon him and seized him and brought him before the council, and they set up false witnesses who said, 'This man never ceases to speak words against this holy place and the law, for we have heard him say that this Jesus of Nazareth will destroy this place and will change the customs that Moses delivered to us.' And gazing at him, all who sat in the council saw that his face was like the face of an angel." Acts 6:8-15.

Stephen was blessed with the gifts of miracles and healing (see Acts 6:8). As we come to chapter 7 of Acts, we'll see the gifts of preaching and teaching being exposed and used in the highest levels of opposition to God's Word and Plan. Again, we see a relatively "uneducated" man exhorting the Scriptures - especially to those who should have known and understood them well - proclaiming God's mercy. Stephen was used specifically by God to do this and I think for an even greater purpose: to serve as a living testimony of what "dying to self" really means.

At the end of chapter 7 of the Book of Acts we read:

"Now when they heard these things they were enraged, and they ground their teeth at him. But he, full of the Holy Spirit, gazed into heaven and saw the glory of God, and Jesus standing at the right hand of God. And he said, 'Behold, I see the heavens opened, and the Son of Man standing at the right hand of God.'

"But they cried out with a loud voice and stopped their ears and rushed together at him. Then they cast him out of the city and stoned him. And the witnesses laid down their garments at the feet of a young man named Saul. And as they were stoning Stephen, he called out, 'Lord Jesus, receive my spirit.' And falling to his knees he cried out with a loud voice, 'Lord, do not hold this sin against them.' And when he had said this, he fell asleep." Acts 7:54-60.

And then there was the Jewish man Saul who became Jesus' apostle and used his legal, Roman name Paul. Saul was a witness to what Stephen had said and done. God was about to do even greater things. Saul had significance through the Sanhedrin and the persecution of the new Church.

Saul believed he was doing God's will and certain that God approved of all he was doing – until he set out for Damascus to search out and persecute Christians. In reality, he was tragically mistaken, opposing the very truth he thought he was defending.

In reality, this was God's Plan for Saul who would become Paul: *"Now as he went on his way, he approached Damascus, and suddenly a light from heaven shone around him. And falling to the ground, he heard a voice saying to him, 'Saul, Saul, why are you persecuting me?' And he said, 'Who are you, Lord?' And he said, 'I am Jesus, whom you are persecuting. But rise and enter the city, and you will be told what you are to do.'"* Acts 9:3-6.

When Saul reached Damascus, God explained to Ananias, one of His believers, something that must have sounded astonishing. God would tell him:

"But the Lord said to him, 'Go, for he is a chosen instrument of mine to carry my name before the Gentiles and kings and the children of Israel. For I will show him how much he must suffer for the sake of my name.'" Acts 9:15-16.

Saul, now Paul, accepted Jesus Christ as his personal Lord and Savior, at which point the Holy Spirit came upon Paul, to dwell in him and endow this ordinary man with extraordinary Spiritual Gifts. Over the next couple of years, the Lord would teach him and then send him out into the world to be His instrument of remarkable change.

In time Paul would use his gifts as an apostle, preacher, teacher, healer, speaker of languages, interpreter of languages, encourager, mentor, and administrator. At various times and in various ways, the Holy Spirit seemed to endow him with all of the Gifts.

And Paul would use all of these Gifts not for his benefit or his own personal significance or relevance, but he would use these Gifts for the furtherance of God's Kingdom and the Gospel of Christ. As each mile of each missionary journey progressed, people - multitudes - would come to Christ. The gentiles would be saved not through the teachings of a Jewish man (not as physically impressive or entertaining as some wanted) who then "saw the light", but they would be moved by the Holy Spirit Himself. Paul was just the mechanism.

Paul was the mechanism to not only reach the gentile world, but to effectively teach it God's Laws and Truths. In his teaching, the great apostle also saw and experienced many of these same Gifts bestowed on the new believers. Paul wanted the believers to grab onto their gifts and use them. The use of Spiritual Gifts helped (and now helps) bring God's order to His Kingdom.

Paul recognized the Gifts of the Spirit and enumerated them in his letters to the Romans and Corinthians. As the letters initially traveled and were shared in the various churches, general knowledge of Spiritual Gifts grew. With the codification of Scripture in the subsequent decades and centuries, we would come to better understand them and their purposes. That's how God works: purposely and orderly.

But that's only the beginning of a discussion of Spiritual Gifts. Whether you read Paul's or Peter's list, they are always framed by an essential question- one that I'll phrase in my own words: *So, what about Spiritual Gifts?*

Both apostles recognized that there's something more important. Paul put it this way in 1 Corinthians 12:31, *"But earnestly desire the higher gifts. And I will show you a still more excellent way."* The explanation would continue in 1 Corinthians 13.

Gifts were and are important, but Godly Love is the greater gift. Our gifts must be used with Love attached. Without love, our Gifts – although given by God – are relatively useless. This is not completely the case, but love puts the real power into the Gifts.

A final observation and "Gift".

As we close this introduction to understanding Spiritual Gifts, there's one last observation that I'd like to make. There's one more "Gift" that needs mentioning. This Gift is not listed with the others. Paul alludes to it, but Peter speaks and writes of it in 1 Peter 4:

"Beloved, do not be surprised at the fiery trial when it comes upon you to test you, as though something strange were happening to you. But rejoice insofar as you share Christ's sufferings, that you may also rejoice and be glad when his glory is revealed. If you are insulted for the name of Christ, you are blessed, because the Spirit of glory and of God rests upon you. But let none of you suffer as a murderer or a thief or an evildoer or as a meddler. Yet if anyone suffers as a Christian, let him not be ashamed, but let him glorify God in that name. For it is time for judgment to begin at the household of God; and if it begins with us, what will be the outcome for those who do not obey the gospel of God? And

"If the righteous is scarcely saved, what will become of the ungodly and the sinner?"

"Therefore let those who suffer according to God's will entrust their souls to a faithful Creator while doing good." 1 Peter 4:12-19.

This last Gift is the Gift of Suffering. Yes, suffering.

Each of the Apostles suffered to the point of death (except John, but even his stories of torture should have killed him). Each of them was willing to put aside their own significance and relevance and die for the sake of the Gospel and the salvation of millions then and hundreds of millions today. In God's eyes and economy, these men and women were completely significant and relevant to His Work.

And each suffered graciously. They knew God had complete control over their lives. Their lives had been crucified so that Christ could live through them (Galatians 2:20). They knew that whatever hardship they would go through was very temporary in light of eternity.

If that's my takeaway for this lesson, so be it. Will I, will you, suffer graciously for the cause and sake of Christ? Will we couple love and suffering with our unique Spiritual Gifts so that others might come to saving knowledge of Jesus?

"But I'm a nobody, I'm just ordinary…"

Yes, we all are until God calls us to a job He wants us to do, and then He empowers us with everything we need to do that job well. Let's go back and look at Saul's conversion on the road to Damascus in Acts 9, and let's specifically look at verses 10 to 18.

10 Now there was a disciple at Damascus named Ananias. The Lord said to him in a vision, "Ananias." And he said, "Here I am, Lord." 11 And the Lord said to him, "Rise and go to the street called Straight, and at the house of Judas look for a man of Tarsus named Saul, for behold, he is praying, 12 and he has seen in a vision a man named Ananias come in and lay his hands on him so that he might regain his sight." 13 But Ananias answered, "Lord, I have heard from many about this man, how much evil he has done to your saints at Jerusalem. 14 And here he has authority from the chief priests to bind all who call on your name." 15 But the Lord said to him, "Go, for he is a chosen instrument of mine to carry my name before the Gentiles and kings and the children of Israel. 16 For I will show him how much he must suffer for the sake of my name." 17 So Ananias departed and entered the house. And laying his hands on him he said, "Brother Saul, the Lord Jesus who appeared to you on the road by which you came has sent me so that you may regain your sight and be filled with the Holy Spirit." 18 And immediately something like scales fell from his eyes, and he regained his sight. Then he rose and was baptized..."

Now, who was Ananias? He was a disciple living in Damascus, about 135 miles (a week's journey in those days) from Jerusalem where the early church was expanding. Ananias was not one of the Apostles living in Jerusalem. Jesus didn't train Ananias. He was out of the limelight. Ananias was, for all practical purposes, a nobody.

And then God called him. And He called him by name. God called Ananias, this nobody disciple living in Damascus, who knew and was likely terrified of Saul. Then in holy obedience, Ananias answered God's call in the same manner that others (think of Moses, Elijah, Elisha, Isaiah, Samuel, and others – all of them "nobodies") answered, "Here I am, Lord."

Like all of us nobodies, Ananias initially answered with excuses of why he couldn't follow through with this divine appointment. But because Ananias was obedient, he went and laid hands on Saul, called him "brother" (that's a surprise in and of itself), and through the power of God, healed his sight. Ananias then had the privilege of baptizing Saul. The Holy Spirit filled Saul with God's power and words so that he could immediately proclaim Jesus as the Son of God.

That was the launching of Saul, who would become Paul, bringing the Gospel of Jesus to the world. Another nobody, Barnabas, would soon enough come alongside Paul in Jerusalem as a witness to the other apostles of what God had done and begun. Barnabas would also become Paul's traveling companion as they traveled into Asia Minor and beyond.

God uses nobodies. We have to remember that when I am weak and believe that I'm not usable by God, He is completely able. Why? Because God has gifted me and you with one or two or perhaps multiple gifts that He will use at His time and place for His purposes. The Bible is replete with "nobodies", and each one of these nobodies God used to change the world and bring people to a saving knowledge of Himself.

You're not, nor ever have been, a nobody! Each of us is created in the image and likeness of God to be used by Him for His purposes, not ours. Most of us will never be known to anyone other than the person we ministered to. Very few of us will be used to bring about unbelievable works in the expansion of God's Kingdom. Use your gifts and answer God's call.

Let's close this lesson in prayer: Heavenly Father, help us to decrease that You might increase so that Jesus is well reflected in our lives. Help us to understand that our Spiritual Gifts are just that, gifts, and that they are gifts from You to be used by You for Your purposes, not ours. You alone are gracious and loving and kind and for that we give You thanks and praise. In the Name of Jesus, we pray. Amen.

Lesson 5 - Peter's Keys to Apologetics

So how did a relatively uneducated, backwoods, backwater fisherman become the first "big name" in Christian apologetics?

It's quite a story! Think about it. A scant three years earlier, this Peter, originally known as Simon, was minding his own business, probably mending his fishing nets for the seemingly millionth time when his brother ran up to him and told him that Messiah had finally come, and Peter needed to meet him. He literally dropped what he was doing and followed Andrew... and the rest is History.

Now Peter just didn't become this fabulous speaker. We read of many times in the Bible where he just plain failed: He spoke when he shouldn't have and then he didn't speak when he should have. At times pride got in the way or his foot got in his mouth. Peter is a normal, mortal man. Sounds like most of us!

The good news is that GOD still chose to use Peter. God, in the Person of Jesus Christ, patiently and personally worked with him day after day, week after week, month after month. And then at some point, GOD knew that Peter was ready. Peter may not have thought so, but God knew. And God knows you and me too.

We have to remember that it is God who is in charge of our lives, not us. He is the one running things. He knows exactly what will or won't work. Our duty is to simply believe, obey, and be available. That's it. If we do these three things, God will work miracles in our lives in the propagation of His Kingdom.

Let's take a closer look at Peter's sermon. It is powerful. It is simple. It is straight forward.

"But Peter, standing with the eleven, lifted up his voice and addressed them: 'Men of Judea and all who dwell in Jerusalem, let this be known to you, and give ear to my words. For these people are not drunk, as you suppose, since it is only the third hour of the day. But this is what was uttered through the prophet Joel:

"'And in the last days it shall be, God declares,
that I will pour out my Spirit on all flesh,
and your sons and your daughters shall prophesy,
   and your young men shall see visions,
   and your old men shall dream dreams;
even on my male servants and female servants
   in those days I will pour out my Spirit, and they shall prophesy.
And I will show wonders in the heavens above
   and signs on the earth below,
   blood, and fire, and vapor of smoke;
the sun shall be turned to darkness
   and the moon to blood,
   before the day of the Lord comes, the great and magnificent day.
And it shall come to pass that everyone who calls upon the name of the Lord shall be saved.'

Peter continues: "Men of Israel, hear these words: Jesus of Nazareth, a man attested to you by God with mighty works and wonders and signs that God did through him in your midst, as you yourselves know — this Jesus, delivered up according to the definite plan and foreknowledge of God, you crucified and killed by the hands of lawless men. God raised him up, loosing the pangs of death, because it was not possible for him to be held by it. For David says concerning him,

"'I saw the Lord always before me,
   for he is at my right hand that I may not be shaken;
therefore my heart was glad, and my tongue rejoiced;
   my flesh also will dwell in hope.
For you will not abandon my soul to Hades,
   or let your Holy One see corruption.
You have made known to me the paths of life;
   you will make me full of gladness with your presence.'

"Brothers, I may say to you with confidence about the patriarch David that he both died and was buried, and his tomb is with us to this day. Being therefore a prophet, and knowing that God had sworn with an oath to him that he would set one of his descendants on his throne, he foresaw and spoke about the resurrection of the Christ, that he was not abandoned to Hades, nor did his flesh see corruption. This Jesus God raised up, and of that we all are witnesses. Being therefore exalted at the right hand of God, and having received from the Father the promise of the Holy Spirit, he has poured out this that you yourselves are seeing and hearing. For David did not ascend into the heavens, but he himself says,

"'The Lord said to my Lord,
"Sit at my right hand,
  until I make your enemies your footstool."'

"Let all the house of Israel therefore know for certain that God has made him both Lord and Christ, this Jesus whom you crucified."

"Now when they heard this they were cut to the heart, and said to Peter and the rest of the apostles, 'Brothers, what shall we do?' And Peter said to them, 'Repent and be baptized every one of you in the name of Jesus Christ for the forgiveness of your sins, and you will receive the gift of the Holy Spirit. For the promise is for you and for your children and for all who are far off, everyone whom the Lord our God calls to himself.' And with many other words he bore witness and continued to exhort them, saying, 'Save yourselves from this crooked generation.' So those who received his word were baptized, and there were added that day about three thousand souls." Acts 2:14-41.

Peter's Five Keys to Apologetics

As we examine this powerful sermon and life-changing event in Acts 2:14 through 41, which impacted thousands of people in Jerusalem nearly 2000 years ago, let's explore what I believe are *Five Keys* that Peter employed in his message. Though Peter may not have been aware of it at the time – he was simply being obedient – his actions provide a model for a strong apologetic, or defense, of the Gospel of Jesus Christ.

First Key: Peter *shows up and stands up* (remember showing up from lesson 1 of this series) with his brothers in Christ. When we stand up with our brothers and sisters in Christ we stand strong. There is strength in numbers. Now granted, as Christians, we are never alone. Christ lives in us, but as we begin to speak to others, especially in larger groups, it's "easier" to have someone back us up. We can be bolder, and this boldness is more than just a shared experience. Those who stand with us are also empowered and encouraged.

Second Key: Peter's knowledge and use of God's Word. Why did Peter speak and quote the Old Testament prophet Joel, chapter 2 verses 28 through 32? I don't really know. But God had a purpose.

Here's that passage in Joel:

"And it shall come to pass afterward,
  that I will pour out my Spirit on all flesh;
your sons and your daughters shall prophesy,
  your old men shall dream dreams,
  and your young men shall see visions.
Even on the male and female servants
  in those days I will pour out my Spirit.

"And I will show wonders in the heavens and on the earth, blood and fire and columns of smoke. The sun shall be turned to darkness, and the moon to blood, before the great and awesome day of the LORD *comes. And it shall come to pass that everyone who calls on the name of the* LORD *shall be saved. For in Mount Zion and in Jerusalem there shall be those who escape, as the* LORD *has said, and among the survivors shall be those whom the* LORD *calls."*

Remember the context of the passage. The event is in Jerusalem. People from all over the Roman Empire had gathered there for the Spring Jewish festivals. These gentiles had all just witnessed the Apostles speaking in their own languages. They truly didn't understand what was happening. In fact, all of Joel chapter 2 is quite eye opening. Back in verses 12 and 13, we are admonished about the proper attitude we should have when worshiping God. Rending garments may "look" holy and pious, but what about our hearts? That's where God wants to work. But back to the passage...

Look through to verse 32 - " *And it shall come to pass that everyone who calls on the name of the LORD shall be saved. For in Mount Zion and in Jerusalem there shall be those who escape, as the LORD has said, and among the survivors shall be those whom the LORD calls.*"

Joel may be a "minor" prophet, but God has given him a major message to be used in these last days; including today. This passage of Scripture was *completely* relevant to Peter's sermon that morning. We also remember that it is God Who does the calling; God does the saving of souls. You and I are merely instruments of His love.

As an aside, recall that Peter's "background" is a Galilean fisherman. He wasn't a scribe. He wasn't a rabbi. He wasn't a "learned" man. He was simply an ordinary man, set aside by God, who was willing to be used by God. He was a man that acknowledged being forgiven and changed by Jesus for a purpose not his own. Peter is not very different from you or me.

How did Peter know all of this stuff? Like any good Jewish boy, he most likely attended services every Sabbath in the local synagogue. He had heard a good amount of the Law and the Prophets growing up. But in the last three years, God Himself taught him. Sitting at Jesus' feet day after day taught him something of God and His Word. More importantly, at this crucial moment, the Holy Spirit empowered and directed Peter and his tongue and by reminding him of everything he *needed* to say. Under His perfect, divine guidance, the Spirit used the mind and heart of Peter to reach the people's hearts. There were no wasted words or ideas. It was exact. The sermon was to the point. God is always succinct; He is never verbose.

Years later, the apostle Paul would pen the words of 2 Timothy 3:16 – 17, summing up the importance and relevance of Scripture: *"All Scripture is breathed out by God and profitable for teaching, for reproof, for correction, and for training in righteousness, that the man* [or woman] *of God may be complete, equipped for every good work."*

Are we diving into God's Word on a regular daily basis in order to know God better and to be "thoroughly equipped"? I ask myself that question all the time.

Third Key: acknowledging God. Throughout this entire passage of Acts chapter 2, God is acknowledged. Remember that as we "defend the faith", God Himself is the very center of that defense. God, as Creator and Sovereign of the Universe must be acknowledged for Who He is and what He has done and what He is doing. The Apostle knew his audience. The Holy Spirit directed his speech as he spoke of God's Sovereignty in the affairs of men. He also acknowledged God's words spoken by His prophets through the ages. He acknowledges God's fulfillment of prophesy. Peter weaves this acknowledgment of God throughout his speech; as should we in our speech.

I believe God wants us to talk about Him all the time. At home, at work, at school. Talking about the Words and Works of God is not something to be saved for Sundays. God is active in our lives 24 hours a day and 7 days a week, every week of the year, without any kind of break. We need to let Him overflow into our lives and speech.

Fourth Key: acknowledge Jesus Christ. In verses 22 to 36, Peter looks at Jesus' life, His works, His atoning death, and most importantly, His Resurrection. Peter recalls what Jesus did in the very midst of the people. Peter recalls how Jesus was referred to by the Old Testament psalms and prophets. The Jews of that time would have heard these readings and texts regardless of their personal leaning - Sadducee (resurrection deniers) or Pharisee (resurrection supporters).

The fact of the time was that Jesus of Nazareth did indeed live, work, and walk among the people. He ministered openly for all to see. Jesus proved His deity through His works. For these few, short years, men and women were actually able to look into the eyes of God Himself. Think about that for just a minute. That's simply astonishing!

Jesus bodily died. But it was not by Jewish stoning (as would have been required for the sin of blasphemy, as charged by the Jewish leaders). It was public Roman crucifixion for all to see. And then to everyone's amazement (despite many denials), Jesus bodily rose from the dead! Remember this: because the resurrected Jesus had appeared to hundreds of people prior to His bodily ascension to heaven after 40 days. Everyone could have gone and asked any of these witnesses. Later on, these same people were willing to die for what they *knew* to be true.

But back to Peter. Peter now had the crowd's attention and as we discussed in the last lesson, this caused them to ask the question, *"Brothers, what shall we do?"* As we speak to friends, neighbors, relatives and anyone God brings into our lives about Christ and His Hope, that should be the question they ask us, "what shall we do?".

Fifth Key: acknowledging our need for a Savior. We need to acknowledge our utter depravity (having broken God's law in rebellion) and our need for Christ (our Savior by faith). Many of us know of someone who is just "really good." They're always honest. They're always helping someone. They don't smoke, drink, chew or "go out with girls (or boys) who do." You know them and you don't think they need to come to a personal relationship with God through the work of Jesus Christ. But we remember that ALL of us have gone astray and sinned, each to his own way; and for that the wrath of God lays heavy on our being (Isaiah 53:6). That means every person who has ever trod this earth, regardless of color, stature or creed. We all have sinned and have fallen short of the Glory of God (Romans 3:23).

And so like Peter, we must direct them to the Savior Jesus Christ. What He did on the Cross cost Him everything. What He offers to us is not only a free gift, but also freedom from sin leading to an eternity of life in proper fellowship and relationship with God. Peter takes the people by the hand and tells them exactly what they must do to be saved: repent from sin (which includes confession), individually (we come alone to the Cross), believe in the finished work of Jesus, receive the gift of forgiveness. Their baptism would demonstrate to the world their inner transformation.

Peter doesn't send them away to seek someone more learned. He calls the people to action. I think Peter understood the idea that years later Paul would pen in his letter to the Corinthians, *"For he says, 'In a favorable time I listened to you, and in a day of salvation I have helped you.' Behold, now is the favorable time; behold, now is the day of salvation."* 2 Corinthians 6:2.

Today is the day of our Salvation. God calls us to be a good and proper witness to the world around us and to those individuals in our sphere of influence. Who will God have you witness to today?

Let's pray: Father God, thank you for giving me the example of the man Peter. Help me to follow Peter's example and use me to bring people to Yourself. Amen.

Lesson 5 – From Doubt to Defense – Peter's Keys to Apologetics

Verses: Acts 2:14 – 41, Joel 2:12 – 13, 32

Key Questions:

How does God use "ordinary" people?

What does God expect of us?

Peter's Model: the "model" presented in Acts 2 demonstrating 5 keys to Apologetics

Why the Old Testament? Joel 2:12 – 13, 32.

Peter's 5 Keys to Apologetics Acts 2: 14 – 41

1. Stand with your brothers & sisters in Christ - verse 14

2. Know God's Word – verses 17 – 21, 25 – 28, 34 - 35

3. Acknowledge God – verses 14 - 41

4. Acknowledge Jesus Christ – verses 22 - 24

5. Acknowledge Our Need – verses 37 – 41

How are we incorporating these 5 keys when we talk to people in the world around us?

Copyright© Ronald Parrs 2025

Follow Peter's Example...

Part 1

As we delve into the study, *From Doubt to Defense*, we come across key models from the apostle Peter that are foundational to our understanding of apologetics. These words provide timeless guidance for defending the Gospel. Let's take some time to unpack these crucial insights.

The first foundational passage is 1 Peter 3:15-16 (we'll look at 2 Peter 3:14-18 in another post). It states, *"but in your hearts honor Christ the Lord as holy, always being prepared to make a defense to anyone who asks you for a reason for the hope that is in you; yet do it with gentleness and respect, having a good conscience, so that, when you are slandered, those who revile your good behavior in Christ may be put to shame."*

Peter went through a lot in his life. You can be sure that this poor - literally - fisherman from the region of Galilee in Judea, never would have dreamed he would be used by God in the way that he was. We can be pretty sure that he was a "good Jew". He feared God. He most likely did all the things that a good Jewish family man would do. He followed, as best as humanly possible, the Law. He attended synagogue. He even presented himself at the Temple in Jerusalem as often as possible.

And then something miraculous happened. By Peter's faith in Jesus Christ, God entered His life and changed it forever. For a time, Peter would be one of the few fortunate people in the history of mankind to actually "touch" God. And God touched him and taught him.

And now as an old man, the Holy Spirit empowered and directed Peter to pen words given to him that would teach men and women for centuries to come. Peter would teach us and prepare us for Jesus' return.

"But..."

Whenever you see the word "but", you really need to ask what it's there for. And so we look back and understand the context of the verse. In 1 Peter chapter 3, the apostle is teaching us about righteous living: wives and husbands; our duties and attitudes toward one another. We are to live harmoniously with each other. And, I believe, not only with respect to our brothers and sisters in Christ, but also with the unbelieving world around us. As Jesus taught Peter and the disciples to be salt and light (Matthew 5:13-14), he passes that same teaching to those listening in the first century and to us today.

Looking back at Acts 2, we see these new people of "the Way" acting and living life in an extraordinary fashion. In fact, we can probably deduce that because they were willing to submit themselves to the apostles' teaching and to one another and to live somewhat communally (freely sharing), the populace around them were taking note. These Christians' lives became living testimonies of the changes God was doing in their lives. As time passed, the unbelievers most likely said to one another, "Hey, I want what they have." Are we, today, living in a like manner?

"...in your hearts set apart Christ as Lord."

We could say that because these first believers had set apart Christ as Lord in their hearts, changes were happening. Their individual and corporate and communal lives were noticeably changing for good - to the glory of God.

The same is true today. Until we have given up the throne in our heart to Jesus and allowed Him to reign as Lord of our lives, we can't be used as God wants us to be used. Could He still use us? Of course. Over the course of history, God has used many unbelievers for His purposes. Nations have risen and fallen by God's Hand on countless, godless leaders. But God gains greater glory when we willingly submit our total being to Him; beginning in our hearts and minds.

As these new believers, armed "only" with the Old Testament and the apostles teaching (which was still being developed), were becoming more Christ-like, they were attracting more and more "seekers" to the Truths of God. But we forget the "invisible" power of the Holy Spirit at work! Nothing happens without the work of the Holy Spirit, whether recognized or not. But that is part of a study unto its own.

"Always be prepared..."

And so, they were "prepared". How else could these people explain their change of life and lifestyle? We remember that many of these folks had not only seen Jesus teach while He lived, they saw Him and learned from Him during that 40-day period after His Resurrection. They were eyewitnesses to the Glorious Risen Christ. They could honestly say something to this effect: "do you remember a few weeks ago at the Passover when..." And, "do you remember that teacher Jesus from Galilee who did (or said) ..." "He is Risen from the dead. I saw Him! I heard Him. My life is changed!"

That's a powerful testimony. Not only was it a good story to tell, but it was also the TRUTH! And that Truth could be corroborated among dozens if not literally hundreds of people.

Today, there are literally millions and millions of people living all around this globe who have been regenerated by and with that same Resurrection power; and our lives are changed as well as those first believers. They have abandoned works-based religiosity for true, faith-based relationship with God through Jesus. We have a similar story to tell. How else can we explain our new lives? We are set free from the sin that ruins us from the inside. We may struggle with certain aspects of sin day in and day out, but it shouldn't have a lasting power over us. We are able to nail that sin to the Cross of Christ and claim His righteousness. Ultimately, in light of Christ's victory, sin is a toothless and defeated foe. At the same time, we recognize that it is indeed His righteousness that saves us and not our own.

Let me be brutally honest with you. When I originally wrote this study, I was struggling with several personal issues. A couple of them were (and continue to be) heart-rending. There was difficulty. There was personal pain. To a certain degree, I had nowhere else to turn except to Jesus and His Cross. Even today, I don't like these difficulties. They are draining in every way. Some of you who know me know of what I refer to (and I covet your friendship and prayer). So, where else would I go? Believe me when I say that I literally have no one or nowhere else to turn to except to Christ. But it is Christ who gives me strength to persevere. I can only trust in Him. I can only pray that God uses this time in my life to bring glory to Himself.

Perhaps you're going through a deep valley in your own life. Perhaps the hurt is so deep and so personal; you don't know where to turn or where to find relief. God knows your every need. He wants you to lean into Him. Proverbs 3:5 - 6 comes to mind,

"Trust in the LORD with all your heart,
   and do not lean on your own understanding.
In all your ways acknowledge him,
   and he will make straight your paths."

As you go through this time, and you will go through it, acknowledge God. Give Him the glory of taking you through it. Present your "reason for the hope that you have." Someone who needs to hear the Good News of Jesus Christ, needs to hear your powerful real-life testimony.

Jesus' Resurrection provides clear and positive and actual Hope for our lives. And as we receive Him as the Savior of our souls and the Lord of our lives, the Holy Spirit then comes in and fills us with the power that we need to not only proclaim these Truths, but the power to live out these Truths. And we boast not in ourselves, "but" (just a fabulous little word) we boast in Christ and His saving power and grace.

"...with gentleness and respect,"

Because the power of Christ, driven by the Holy Spirit, is able to do these things - words and deeds - we are able to deliver a message with a powerful gentleness and respect that is otherwise impossible. The writer of Proverbs 15:1 - 2 says it correctly:

"A soft answer turns away wrath,
   but a harsh word stirs up anger.
The tongue of the wise commends knowledge,
   but the mouths of fools pour out folly."

God wants us to speak truthfully about what He is doing in our lives. He doesn't necessarily want us to air all of our dirty laundry, but He does want us to be truthful about our condition and about what He is doing about it and with it. This is not a snarky, "what's true for me isn't necessarily true for you," thing. It's what is true. Period. Here are the facts. Believe them as you see them. This is how God is working in my life. Our testimony is an individual testimony, a personal testimony. No one can take that away from you.

"...so that, when you are slandered, those who revile your good behavior in Christ may be put to shame."

So that in everything, Christ is magnified and glorified. He alone is worthy of Glory and Honor. The fact of the matter is we will be slandered for the cause and sake of Jesus. Jesus Himself said that He would be a stumbling block to many. And so, He is. Foolish men and women who choose to live a life apart from God will surely mock us. It's inevitable.

But all that God has asked us to do is be a witness for Him. We are to speak well of our Savior. We are to act as Jesus did and would act. We are to bring, by His power and Spirit, life into a dying world. He died so that we may live; and even more, to live abundantly! Maybe not necessarily in this life now, but when we step into eternity we will be welcomed as heirs of His Kingdom.

For those who choose not to turn to Christ: that is to their own peril and destruction. We cannot drag people into the Kingdom against their will. They themselves have to bend the knee and the heart to God in repentance and submission. They have to seek forgiveness from God. We can only speak of the Truthful work He has done in our own lives. We are to give a "reason for the hope" that we have.

In the end, as redeemed and regenerated and restored men and women, we should be reflecting the glory and grace of God. We have a story to tell of the Hope we have because of our rebirth; because of our new birth. He has remade us to be beautiful; and beauty is attractive. True - from the inside out - beauty is stunning and desirable. When we are beautiful, as in Christ, God shows us off as His workmanship and attracts others to Himself.

This is our mission: Share Christ and the good work He has done in our lives. That, my friends, is the undeniable answer we are to give, with gentleness and respect, to a world that is looking for not only answers, but redemption.

Continue to Follow Peter's Example

Part 2

One thing we know about the apostle Peter, he spoke frankly...

In the Gospels, we often find Peter getting ahead of himself. He had, I believe, a touch of "foot in mouth" disease. Whether it was defending Jesus or wanting to build a memorial to Him or wanting to walk on water with His Savior, Peter seemed to speak or act first, then dealt with the consequences later.

Most of us suffer from this human ailment from time to time. Usually, it was Jesus Himself that reeled the disciple back in and lovingly instructed him. And as he aged and matured, he began doing as he was taught by the Master. He thought first, then prayed, then finally spoke.

2 Peter 3:14 - 18, is the second foundational verse for our study of *From Doubt to Defense*. We looked at 1 Peter 3:15 - 16 last time, and we were able to glean quite a bit from those two verses when it came to the subject of apologetics.

These verses in 2 Peter chapter 3 are a bit more direct in making his appeal that we believers are personally and individually responsible for understanding the Scriptures and presenting them in a cogent way to the unbelieving world around us. Peter even invokes the apostle Paul and his writing to be used and studied in the defense of the Christian Faith.

Before we dive into the passage, let's take a look at the context. 2 Peter is his second and last epistle. Whereas 1 Peter dealt with pressures from outside the church, 2 Peter deals with the problems and pressures that had already infiltrated the fledgling church. Misunderstandings - both accidental and purposeful - were coming into the pulpit and causing confusion among the believers and church goers. The foxes were already getting into the chicken coop. As chapter 3 of 2 Peter unfolds, Peter is discussing the final return of Jesus Christ in the future. And even though we look forward to this event, we need to be diligent and on guard with our thinking, speaking and actions. We are to continue proclaiming Christ and his finished work at the cross, and we are to seek Godly wisdom with all that we do.

Here is the passage, 2 Peter 3:14 - 18,

"Therefore, beloved, since you are waiting for these, be diligent to be found by him without spot or blemish, and at peace. And count the patience of our Lord as salvation, just as our beloved brother Paul also wrote to you according to the wisdom given him, as he does in all his letters when he speaks in them of these matters. There are some things in them that are hard to understand, which the ignorant and unstable twist to their own destruction, as they do the other Scriptures. You therefore, beloved, knowing this beforehand, take care that you are not carried away with the error of lawless people and lose your own stability. But grow in the grace and knowledge of our Lord and Savior Jesus Christ. To him be the glory both now and to the day of eternity. Amen."

Let's break it down.

"…since you are waiting for these,"

What are we looking forward to or waiting for? We're looking forward to the new heaven and new earth that God will bring at the end of the age. We want to look forward to Jesus coming again and the righteousness that He will restore to all of His creation. That's an amazing thing. And when it happens, it will happen in a timely and rapid way.

When you read Revelation 21 and of the new heaven and new earth coming down, it is not taking billions and billions of years. The initial Creation was done by God in six literal days, why would the new, redeemed Creation take any longer? All of creation, all sentient (being self-aware) beings whether redeemed or condemned will witness God's power as He remakes and restores everything for His glory. Keep this in mind when we look at worldviews and apologetic strategies; especially when dealing with the topic of evolution and creation.

But back to the text.

"…be diligent to be found by him without spot or blemish, and at peace."

In other words, we are to live, speak and function in a way that gives glory to God - the "him" in that part of the verse. It will take effort. Peter doesn't gloss over that fact. You could almost make the leap that Peter knows that we will sometimes fail in those efforts. That is normal for fallen men and women. Peter knew that. Peter even experienced that fact time and time again.

He knows - even God knows - that we cannot live sinless lives, but we can take on the responsibility to make every effort to live a life that is pleasing to God and that will attract the unbeliever. We are not to live a false piety or to lord our redeemed lives over the unbeliever because we were all once like them: an enemy of God.

"Bear in mind that our Lord's patience..."

God is long suffering as He brings salvation to His creation. Time is on His side. God will not act, Christ will not come again, until all and every last person is saved and His prophesies are fulfilled, according to HIS plan. We don't know the time and day. God does, and we are to be ready and not just waiting.

But this is where we need to be focused on the Gospel. This is where we need to understand God's Word and God's Wisdom as presented in the Bible. We are not to take His Word out of context for our own purposes. We are to use His Word to lead people to a saving knowledge of Jesus Christ. The Bible is both the Foundation for the defense of the Faith and the Defense of the Faith itself.

"... our beloved brother Paul also wrote to you "

The Bible is always supporting itself. Peter knew Paul. In the beginning, he probably feared Paul; and then God transformed this man who was actively persecuting the Church into a "tool" that He would use to bring His Gospel to the world. Peter recognizes that Paul is not only scholarly in his writings, but that the wisdom that he writes of comes from God Himself. Once "enemies", these two men are now brothers in Christ. That is a demonstration of the reconciling power of the Cross.

Peter continues to direct the fledgling church to seek God and to use the writings of Paul as its guide. Paul's writings may be "difficult" to understand, but we are to use them nonetheless. It is our responsibility to read and study God's Word and as we read and study it, it becomes a part of thinking and of our lives. Peter knows that the Spirit will provide the wisdom and the guidance to come to an understanding of God and His ways.

"...which the ignorant and unstable twist to their own destruction, as they do the other Scriptures..."

This really is the crux of the matter, isn't it? The early Church struggled with the Scriptures then as we do today. People come in, claiming to be believers or followers of Christ and yet they are truly not. Now I know that may sound terribly judgmental, but we need to be cognizant of the "fruit" of these believers, don't we? How many people take Scripture out of its context to make it say what they believe or want others to believe? When that happens, the world is confused and God and His Message of true Salvation is grossly distorted (even if the distortion is "minor", it is still a gross distortion) and not True.

Today, we see distortions such as Westboro Baptist Church and their ungracious attitude toward the families of our soldiers as one example. Another was the "impending" Day of Judgment, May 21, 2011. That day has obviously come and gone... Then there is the segment of teachers (notably Rob Bell formerly of Mars Hill Bible Church in Michigan - not to be confused with Mark Driscoll formerly of Mars Hill Church in Seattle, Washington) who are actively denying hell using God's love and beneficence to preclude a literal hell and eternal damnation (also notice that these people will claim that they are teaching the Bible by even using the word "bible" in the name of their organization). In the end, God Himself will judge these people. The men and women who lead the flock astray will be dealt with most severely.

Today we continue in the twisting of the Scriptures as "progressive Christianity" and the full-fledged acceptance of the LGBTQ plus (including the mutilation of children) agenda in many mainline denominations. We have been called to love, but before that, Jesus calls *us* to repentance.

God wants us to deal truthfully in all matters of life, but most importantly when it comes to preaching and teaching His Word. Do I fear God in these matters? Yes, I do. Any of us who teach and preach His Word, I believe, are held to a higher standard. We are to be diligent in what we write and say, so as to not lead anyone astray.

"You therefore, beloved, knowing this beforehand, take care..."

I think that goes without saying... One thing that I have always appreciated about the pastors of my home church is that they continually admonish all of us sitting in the congregation to prove what they speak from the pulpit directly with the Bible. Period. In that way, we are on our guard. God holds us personally responsible for "working out our salvation" (Phil 2:12).

If we are not on our guard, we can easily be swayed. The words of influential men and women can tickle the ear. Our sinful nature wants to hear what it wants to hear. Sometimes God's Word is hard. Sometimes God's Word does cut us to the heart. We remember Hebrews 4:12, *"For the word of God is living and active, sharper than any two-edged sword, piercing to the division of soul and of spirit, of joints and of marrow, and discerning the thoughts and intentions of the heart."*

If your pastor or Sunday school teacher says something that doesn't seem right, pray. Then open your Bible (if you haven't already) and study. If it still doesn't seem right, speak with your pastor or teacher about the issue. Perhaps there was or is a misunderstanding; perhaps not. God Himself will speak the Truth.

We believers need to stay (abide) in His Word daily. Read the difficult passages of Scripture. If you don't understand them, that's okay. Petition the Holy Spirit to open your mind and heart to what He wishes - or chooses - to teach you. Maybe it's a passage that He may not "want" you to understand at this particular time. God and His Word can never be fully known. That's why it will take eternity to get to know Him!

"But grow in the grace and knowledge of our Lord..."

That is what we are to do. Being "in" Christ, we are fed by the Holy Spirit. He alone wins the battles of and for our hearts and minds - if we allow Him. As we willingly submit, the Spirit fills us to overflowing with His Grace and His Knowledge. That is the power that overcomes and truly changes the world; nothing else comes close. Our pitiful human words and actions may "cause" some minor changes, but it is God and His moving that shakes the world to its foundations.

Grace is God's power in action. That is the best way I can describe it. It is an awesome power. Knowledge is useful, but it is grace - God's Grace - that is the true power (you can plug into the Attributes of Grace Study).

And so to sum this all up, Peter again speaks frankly. Peter says it best,

"To Him be the glory both now and to the day of eternity. Amen."

Amen!

Lift your eyes to God and His Word. Be bold. Speak His Truths to those God has placed in your particular sphere of influence. That's what He has called you and me to do.

The Unbelieving Mind

The Christian is in a knock-down, drag-out war with the culture around us.

The worst part of the battle is the constant double-standard foisted upon us. When we believers call for a return to morals and Godliness, we have to hold a mirror up to our own lives first. And when we stumble and fall, we're (Christians) at least willing to admit our wrong doing (sometimes), seek forgiveness and repent or turn toward Godliness.

Unbelievers, for the most part, wave the red flag of guilt in our faces, reminding us of the standard we are to be following and adhering to. But when it comes to their sin - yes, let's just call it that - out come the excuses. The omission, the "I didn't know", the "well everybody else is doing it".

And we Christians are called the "hypocrites".

I don't know about you, but I'm tired.

But I'm not going to give up. If anything, as I engage the culture around me, I have greater resolve to understand my adversary's mind. The apostle Paul helps me to understand the unbeliever. And even though his words are almost two thousand years old, they are as pertinent and applicable today thanks to the power and inspiration of the Holy Spirit. The words are blunt. The words are clear. Let's look at this very hard-hitting passage, as we come to an understanding of the unbelieving mind in Romans chapter one.

Paul writes in the first chapter of the epistle to the Romans, *"For the wrath of God is revealed from heaven against all ungodliness and unrighteousness of men, who by their unrighteousness suppress the truth. For what can be known about God is plain to them, because God has shown it to them. For his invisible attributes, namely, his eternal power and divine nature, have been clearly perceived, ever since the creation of the world, in the things that have been made. So they are without excuse. For although they knew God, they did not honor him as God or give thanks to him, but they became futile in their thinking, and their foolish hearts were darkened.*

Claiming to be wise, they became fools, and exchanged the glory of the immortal God for images resembling mortal man and birds and animals and creeping things.

"Therefore God gave them up in the lusts of their hearts to impurity, to the dishonoring of their bodies among themselves, because they exchanged the truth about God for a lie and worshiped and served the creature rather than the Creator, who is blessed forever! Amen." Romans 1:18-25.

We Christians have to understand this passage well. The Holy Spirit, writing through Paul, unveils the unbeliever's mind so that we can better know our enemy. We are in this battle to bring glory to God as He uses us to engage our culture. We engage them sometimes face to face. At other times we may engage them via email or in blogs and even online chat rooms and other social media. But we must engage them. As painful as this passage is - for we were once unbelievers - we need to unpack it.

We unpack it to not only gain an understanding of the unbelievers in our circles of influence, but to be reminded from where God has graciously delivered us.

"For the wrath of God is revealed..."

Indeed, it is. And it is frightful. People want to have and "enjoy" a God of love and peace, but they don't "like" a God of wrath and judgment. They don't think it's "fair" that God could be wrathful. The fact of the matter is that if they don't like God's wrath now, just wait for the real judgment to come. Too many believe that they're going to heaven because God is loving, but they don't want to believe that He is also Holy and His standard is perfection (the perfection as demonstrated in the life of Jesus). They find it acceptable for a Hitler or Stalin or Saddam Hussein or Osama bin Laden to be cast into an eternal hell, but for the simple "denier of Christ", that's completely unacceptable.

Now you may think I'm a little off or a bit crazy, but we see God's wrath all around us. Whether it's the AIDS epidemic (choosing to live and participate in a less than optimal lifestyle) or famine (the "man-caused" type some of them exacerbated by certain political regimes who desire to defeat their enemies who are their own countrymen) or natural disasters such as the earthquakes and tsunamis that we have witnessed (*"We know that the whole creation has been groaning as in the pains of childbirth right up to the present time."* Romans 8:22). And God is not going to be letting up any time soon. God is reminding all of creation Who He is and Who is in charge.

"...**men, who by their unrighteousness suppress the truth**."

This is the truth of the matter. Men and women, as much as they will deny this, don't want God in their lives. They don't want truth. God's Truth interferes with their "fun" and lifestyle. Our constant trafficking in sin, no matter how grievous or "minor" suppresses God's truth. And the suppression of true truth begins in our minds.

The noetic effects (the way that "sin negatively affects and undermines our minds and intellect") of sin on our person strip us not only of our humanity but corrupts our image. We humans have been created in God's image (remember that only mankind is created in the image of God, not even angels can claim that). We are His image bearers. But as sin corrupts our minds, the rest of our image becomes distorted and corrupt. We might as well be looking at ourselves in fun-house mirrors.

The noetic effects of sin results in hardened hearts and lives that are set directly against our Creator. And although God has given us every opportunity to know and experience Him at every turn of our daily walk, we ignore Him. We ignore His Truths. We suppress the Truth by our personal wickedness. We suppress God's Truth by constantly forcing it away and out of our sight. We know what we ought to do but don't do it. We believe we know better. In our own minds, we believe we know better than God. We consciously and unconsciously push God aside. Ultimately, we, like Satan, want to be seated on God's throne. We are without excuse as Paul reminds us in verse 20.

"**For although they knew God**..."

And that's the rub. We know God, at least in the "acquainted with" sense. Not to be crude, but the unbeliever doesn't know - or purposefully chooses not to know - God in the Biblical sense. The unbeliever - the atheist, the agnostic, whatever moniker you wish to give them -

purposefully chooses to deny or at least to ignore God. They deny their dependence upon Him. They believe they lead "liberated" lives by cutting the tether to their Creator.

As believers in Jesus Christ, in God, we do know Him in the biblical sense. We are in an eternal relationship. He knows us - you and me - intimately. He desires the same for us; that we would come to know Him intimately. Hopefully, we believers do give Him thanks and praise. As our relationship deepens, we trust Him more. We give Him glory for all that He is and does in our lives.

But the unbeliever, does not. And the further the suppression, the greater the gulf of separation. In time, the thinking becomes futile (verse 21). Futility turns into foolishness and then foolishness leads to a darkened heart. Take a look at Psalm 94:

"Understand, O dullest of the people!
Fools, when will you be wise?
He who planted the ear, does he not hear?
He who formed the eye, does he not see?
He who disciplines the nations, does he not rebuke?
He who teaches man knowledge—
the LORD—knows the thoughts of man,
that they are but a breath." Psalm 94:8-11.

"Claiming to be wise..."

How many so-called "wise" people do you know of are actually "fools"? That's a rhetorical question. You don't have to answer that. But the truth remains. Psalm 14:1 says it best, "*The fool says in his heart, 'There is no God.' They are corrupt, they do abominable deeds; there is none who does good.*" It's always a "heart and mind" thing. There's only about 12 inches or so between the two and they do influence each other.

God wants us to use our minds. He knows that our hearts are deceitful above all (Jeremiah 17:9). The heart deals with feelings and emotions. That's not entirely bad, but we have to temper those feelings and emotions with the rational thinking that the mind provides; that God provides. That's how God operates. Created in His image, God has communicated to us - all human beings - many of His attributes including emotions and reason.

The problem is that when we neglect the proper use of our minds to acknowledge good and evil, right and wrong, righteousness and unrighteousness, we eventually deny most, if not all of the majesty and glory of God. Instead, we cling to corruption. We worship the created things - you name it, even our own desires - rather than the Creator. In reality, even the atheist creates his or her own "god" to worship, cherish and adore with all of their heart, mind, spirit, and personal strength, not recognizing that they are paving a highway to eternal punishment and separation from the true God of the universe.

In the end, our demanding spirit and attitude desires only that which is man-made. We exchange all of the beauty and majesty of God for trifles. At long last, in many instances - too many instances - God "acquiesces" and says, "Okay, you want it, you've got it. I'll give it to you in spades." This is the hardened heart that the Scriptures have warned against… to their ultimate peril.

"Therefore, God gave them up..."

We've reached bottom. To the unbelieving mind and person though, it may seem that they have arrived. They've reached the pinnacle of their desires. They have it all. All of the sinful desires are theirs for the keeping, for the enjoying… or so they think.

In another lesson I wrote something to the effect that the unsaved, unbelieving person believes that they're off to this great big party with their buddies in Hell. How wrong they are… and how sad. They denied God foolishly thinking that they had plenty of time to repent. But then it's too late. The righteous judgment of God will be meted out. Mercy and grace, although extended for years and years, will be withdrawn and they will reap their reward of iniquity and final and eternal separation from God who offered them literally everything for eternity.

That is our battle. That is the culture war we have been called to engage in.

As we engage in "apologetics", we engage the minds and hearts of our families, our friends, and our co-workers. God has provided each one of us with the tools that we need in order to make that difference as we understand the unbeliever. We enter into conversation with them to tell them the Good News of God and hopefully - if God wills it for us - we will emerge with a "new" friend of God. We do not have the power to change their mind, only God has that power. Only He can bring them out of their self-determined wilderness leading to destruction. We will have been faithful with our message, guided by the Holy Spirit, that is able to prove to them the loving faithfulness of God.

Will we accept the assignment God has given us? Will we make the time and spend time in Bible reading and study and prayer to prepare ourselves to meet with and engage the unbeliever? Will we open our mouths and speak His Truth to the best of our ability, allowing the Holy Spirit to work through us?

Not only are we challenged to accept the assignment of engaging the world around us, but how will we do it? Will we be winsome and loving and caring? Will we take the time to walk alongside them, loving them for who they are? Will we refuse to sacrifice our standards and instead hold them high enough to be godly but low enough that we understand that they are as filthy rags in God's sight? Will we love them the way Jesus loves them? Will we allow GOD to do the saving? We are powerless. He is all powerful.

The really good news is that we know Who our Champion is. The believer is on the side of victory already. The Resurrection of Jesus Christ is the promise of that Victory.

Lord God, our gracious and loving Father, thank you for allowing us to take part in Your battle for the souls of Your creation, Your children. We pray that You provide us with the right words and the right attitude to engage the unbelieving world around us. Use each and every one of Your saints for Your glory alone. Fill us with Your Holy Spirit. Fill us with Your Truth. Let only Your Words of Life come from our lips as we engage a lost world. Amen.

Lesson 6 - Practical Preaching

Here's the rub: Are we walking the walk or just talking the talk? If it's the latter, that's "look-good" Christianity. That's not what God has called us to.

This is probably the biggest struggle we Christians have. We can do 99 things right, but the ONE thing we flub, that's what is noticed by the unbelieving world.

As Chapter 2 of the Book of the Acts of the Apostles draws to a close, the Evangelist Luke gives us a word picture snapshot of the day-to-day life of the new Christian believers in Jerusalem. This snapshot provides every believer with how we should be conducting our lives, becoming a natural attraction to the unbelieving world. Let's look at how we ought to live using verses 42 through 47 as a guide.

Acts 2:42-47 reads: *"And they devoted themselves to the apostles' teaching and the fellowship, to the breaking of bread and the prayers. And awe came upon every soul, and many wonders and signs were being done through the apostles. And all who believed were together and had all things in common. And they were selling their possessions and belongings and distributing the proceeds to all, as any had need. And day by day, attending the temple together and breaking bread in their homes, they received their food with glad and generous hearts, praising God and having favor with all the people. And the Lord added to their number day by day those who were being saved."*

The early Christians practiced three general "walks." They were Devoted. They Gave. And they Praised (worshipped).

Devotion is a must. Whatever we do, we had better be devoted to it. Devotion is, or at least should be, an all or nothing proposition. Whether it's to a person (our spouse and children), a cause, our work. We should be wanting to give our all. In this case of Acts chapter 2, the believers were devoted not only to God and what He had done, but also to the Apostles (God's earthly teachers), their teaching and to prayer.

I think we can read between the lines and say that the people loved and cared for the Apostles. The people realized that the Apostles had been taught by God Himself in the person of Jesus. By being devoted to the teaching of the Apostles, they willingly put themselves under the authority of the Twelve. Their new lives were completely dependent upon God's Word as their complete sustenance. The Apostles taught them how to pray, not as the "learned" priests, scribes and Pharisees, but as people utterly dependent upon God; praying in Spirit and in Truth.

There is a difference between "knowing about" God and "knowing" God. The former is usually learned through books and sermons and videos and anything else you can think of that is "about" the Bible. There's nothing wrong with these tools in and of themselves, but it's not the same. In order to know God, you have to know His Word - the Bible - and be in it by reading it on a daily and regular basis. How do you "know" someone if you only read or listen to snippets or hearsay? You get to know someone by spending time with them – significant time.

We Christians receive a lot of blame (some of it rightly so) for certain persecutions or bad times over the centuries. But what about all of the good that the Christian Church has done? What about the institutions of higher learning and hospitals? What about the ending of slavery in the Western world. All of those things were promoted and promulgated by Christians.

We are devoted to our Savior and desire to share the same gifts he has shared with us. We devote our lives to Him and to those He has placed over us as our pastors, priests and teachers. As long as Christ is first, there is nothing wrong in devoting yourself to another person.

Not only were they devoted to the Apostles, but they also devoted themselves to one another. They met regularly together to pray and for fellowship. They encouraged one another. Let's face it; these people were most likely looked upon as being "weird"; kind of how the world perceives Christian believers even today. Peter perhaps put it best by calling us "peculiar" (1 Peter 2:9, KJV); yes we are.

In giving, the believers gave. They gave to anyone. They gave to one another first, then to the neighbors and neighborhoods around them. When God placed a need in their midst, they gave to provide for that need. This type of giving must have seemed extraordinary. Many years ago,

I served as the financial secretary of our church. To say that it was a humbling experience is an understatement; and that's all that I will say.

Even today, whenever there is an emergency at home or abroad; natural or man-made, Christians GIVE. And it's not just money. It's a giving of time, effort, love for fellow man no matter what the circumstances are. Hurricane Katrina hit the Gulf Coast of the United States in August of 2005. My home church and many others are still sending in volunteers to help with restoring life years later after the government has left. We see doctors literally giving their lives to minister to Muslims in Afghanistan; these people would otherwise not have special medical care. There are teachers going into the war-torn areas of the world providing education which then provides hope to hundreds and thousands of illiterate people. Giving is one of the attributes of Grace and Grace is something that separates Christians from unbelievers.

Finally, these Acts chapter 2 Christians praised God. I must believe that praising God was part of their everyday speech. These believers wore God on their sleeves. They were supremely grateful for what He had done in their lives; and they wanted to share it with everyone. Is that how we live our lives? Are we so thankful for all that God has done in our lives that we want to shout it from the rooftops for all the world to hear and see? Or do we allow the world to smother our Joy and remain silent?

I have known, like you, good times and bad; times of ease as well as times of hardship. In those "easy" times, I tend to "forget" about God and His provision. I put myself on cruise control and go about my life. But when the going gets tough, I run out to find my Savior. He wants me with Him at all times, not just in fiery furnace, but every day.

I remember once telling a pastor friend of mine about a very difficult financial situation. What did he tell me to do aside from praying? "Praise Him first and present an offering. Thank Him for ALL that you have." I did. The situation didn't magically go away, but my attitude changed and God brought me through the difficulty with His grace, and perhaps some unbelievers noticed.

And I am to praise Him for everything. I enter His gates with a thankful heart and voice.

Here's the result of this "Christian activity."

The world around us is actively searching for Hope and Love and Grace. God has called each one of us to Praise HIM and give Glory to Him and to point others to Him. God wants us to be fragrant and attractive to the world around us. All of us are called to be extensions of Christ in a sinful and weary world. And in that way, God brings the lost to Himself and saves them. *"…the Lord added to their number day by day those who were being saved."* Acts 2:47

In Richard Pratt's book, *"Every Thought Captive"* he begins with the understanding that as we believers present a defense of the Gospel, it is God's Word that we are defending AND that we USE God's Word as our primary defense. Nothing else will do. God's Word must be the foundation to our "apologia;" just like those first, early believers. They may not have had the Bible as we do now, but they had the Law, the Prophets, the Psalms. They also had the Holy Spirit living in them and guiding them to remember the Words of Jesus.

May we follow them well in their footsteps.

Lesson 6 – From Doubt to Defense – Practical Preaching

Verses: Acts 2:42 – 47

Key Questions:

How do we "walk the walk"?

How do we "talk the talk"?

How do we walk and talk?

As you look at Acts 2:42 – 47, discuss the how the 3 general "Walks" were accomplished.

1. Devotion -
a. to God

b. to our Church leaders

c. to one another

2. Giving -
a. to God

b. to our Church leaders

c. to one another

3. Praise -
a. personal life

b. public life

The Foundation: How are you making the Bible your firm foundation?

Copyright© Ronald Parrs 2025

Lesson 7 - Right Relationship

So, if God is the Creator, I'm the creature.

As we study and practice apologetics, we have to not only start on the right foot, we have to understand what our "worldview" is. A worldview is just that: HOW we, as an individual, look at the world around us and our actions in it. Our worldview(s) color literally everything else that we think about, speak about, and react to. As Christians, we have definite, often times opposing, worldviews as compared to non-Christians, wiccans, atheists, agnostics, and other post-modernists.

What we believe about God and Who He is and how we relate to Him forms the foundation of our worldview. But it is not enough to argue for the "simple" existence of God, or theism. As believers, we are to defend Christian Theism. That is the belief in God as the Tri-une Being of Father, Son and Holy Spirit.

I know that's a big order, but to that point, we begin.

Our foundation *must* begin with a clear understanding of who God is. True, biblical, orthodox (right thinking) Christianity - alas, even the Bible itself - asserts two essential facts about God: He created all things, and He is Tri-une in nature. Before we wrap our brains around the Truth of God existing all of the time and simultaneously in the persons of Father, Son and Holy Spirit, let's get a little more basic.

In Job chapters 38 through 41, God quizzes Job about the known universe and everything in it. Did Job have any part in creation? No.

"Where were you when I laid the foundation of the earth?
  Tell me, if you have understanding.
Who determined its measurements—surely you know!
  Or who stretched the line upon it?
On what were its bases sunk,
  or who laid its cornerstone,

when the morning stars sang together
   and all the sons of God shouted for joy?

"Or who shut in the sea with doors
   when it burst out from the womb," Job 38:4-8

How about Job being able to control behemoth or leviathan? No again. Job was mortal. He was born and then he died.

"Behold, Behemoth,
   which I made as I made you;
   he eats grass like an ox.
Behold, his strength in his loins,
   and his power in the muscles of his belly.
He makes his tail stiff like a cedar;
   the sinews of his thighs are knit together.
His bones are tubes of bronze,
   his limbs like bars of iron.

"He is the first of the works of God;
   let him who made him bring near his sword!" Job 40:15-19

The REAL foundation that we begin with is that God is the Creator of ALL things. And that means ALL things: every star and planet, every rock and tree, every fish and bird, every person, every atom and its subatomic parts. God is the perfect and reasonable explanation for all that is. With that foundation, I can state my beliefs simply and succinctly. Period.

Furthermore, without God NOTHING can exist. He brought it all into existence. He can take it all out of existence whenever He wants. He holds everything together. God is only responsible to Himself. He colors the New England autumn leaves as He likes as much as He colors the various nebulae in the sky. Order and beauty abound in all things He has created. More than a finely crafted watch or the intricacy of the human eye, there is order, beauty and even function and purpose (a key word and strategy that we'll cover much later). All of it exists for HIS glory and HIS pleasure. God allows us the opportunity of sharing all of this with all of us. God is a "relational" Being; relationships are His thing. But there is also a hierarchy in Creation.

And what about us? We are the creature. Man did not "create" God (although certain philosophies would suggest just that) in his image. No, God created US in HIS image (Genesis 1:26). Male and female, He created us. Whereas the universe and seas and plants and animals were spoken into existence by His Word, man was crafted out of the dust of the earth and when properly formed, God breathed His Spirit into man, passing on to us His communicable attributes.

We are dependent upon God for Four general areas: Physical, Historical, Knowledge, and Morality.

Man is dependent upon God Physically.

But we are still the creature. Man and woman is still 100% dependent upon God for everything. Psalm 139:13-16 reads:

"For you formed my inward parts;
  you knitted me together in my mother's womb.
I praise you, for I am fearfully and wonderfully made.
Wonderful are your works;
  my soul knows it very well.
My frame was not hidden from you,
when I was being made in secret,
  intricately woven in the depths of the earth.
Your eyes saw my unformed substance;
in your book were written, every one of them,
   the days that were formed for me,
   when as yet there was none of them."

As independent as we may want to be, it is only God who is truly independent. We need air. God doesn't. We need food and drink. God doesn't. He always existed and always will exist. We men and women had a beginning; God didn't. The other side of that coin is that none of us will have an end – we will either end in glory for eternity or damnation for eternity.

We depend on God for our History.

By the work of the Holy Spirit, we see God's guiding hand throughout history. Where we came from, where we're going. In Acts chapter 7, we see the church's first martyr Stephen arguing before the Jewish Sanhedrin. Stephen eloquently, under the influence of the Holy Spirit, lays out Israel's history. From Abraham and Isaac and Jacob and Joseph to Moses to finally King David and his son Solomon. History is truly God's History. It's His-story. God was in the details then and is in the details today.

The Bible is not just a book of fairy tales as many unbelievers say it is. The Bible and authenticity to historical events have been proven time and time again. Archaeology is continually digging up (pardon the pun), new and more relevant pieces of the puzzle of history that support the Bible. The people mentioned in the Bible are actual historical men and women, kings and queens, heroes and villains. Extra-biblical writing proves them correct. Even certain prophecies of the Old Testament writers have found credence with support from other historians such as Josephus and others.

Romans 15:4, sums it up nicely, *"For whatever was written in former days was written for our instruction, that through endurance and through the encouragement of the Scriptures we might have hope."*

Man should be learning from his past actions and mistakes. We can more effectively move forward by examining what was behind us.

We depend on God for knowledge.

We don't know everything and for that reason we keep searching.

God is omniscient. God wants His creation to KNOW Him. God makes Himself known to us in two ways: through General Revelation and Special Revelation.

General Revelation is what God provides, by Grace, to every man, woman and child on the planet, no matter what their individual stature. We can know God and gain knowledge just by looking at and examining the world and universe around us. God calls out to His creation to know Him. God essentially "lays Himself bare" for all to see in the general revelation of creation itself. We can know God just by looking out the window. Psalm 19:1 states, *"The heavens declare the glory of God, and the sky above proclaims his handiwork."*

Then there is God's Special Revelation. We see God's hand weaving through history as He drives it to an eventual conclusion. God specifically draws attention to Himself through the special revelation of the Old and New Testaments of the Bible. He beckons all men and women to read, drink in and get to know Him. In the person of Jesus Christ, man was able to actually touch God for the very first time; to hold Him as a baby, to break bread with Him, to touch His resurrected body. Hebrews 1:1-2, say it well: *"Long ago, at many times and in many ways, God spoke to our fathers by the prophets, but in these last days he has spoken to us by his Son, whom he appointed the heir of all things, through whom also he created the world."*

Jesus goes on to speak to us specifically in John 6:44-51,

"No one can come to me unless the Father who sent me draws him. And I will raise him up on the last day. It is written in the Prophets, 'And they will all be taught by God.' Everyone who has heard and learned from the Father comes to me— not that anyone has seen the Father except he who is from God; he has seen the Father. Truly, truly, I say to you, whoever believes has eternal life. I am the bread of life. Your fathers ate the manna in the wilderness, and they died. This is the bread that comes down from heaven, so that one may eat of it and not die. I am the living bread that came down from heaven. If anyone eats of this bread, he will live forever. And the bread that I will give for the life of the world is my flesh."

This is an incredibly bold statement. He tells us that we can know - truly know – God by knowing Him. Unfortunately, most of the world rejects this statement. It is too narrow; it isn't fair. The Jews (unbelievers) grumbled then when Jesus spoke these words, and many more grumble today.

We depend on God for a standard of morality.

When left to our own devices, all men become immoral and corrupt – but not because we were originally created that way. Rather, we inherit a sin nature from Adam's fall, a nature inclined toward rebellion against God. However, while this fallen nature predisposes us to sin, we are each personally responsible for our own sins – our own choices that make us morally guilty before God. He alone is the perfect standard of morality embodying justice, mercy, love, righteous anger, and wrath. How an atheist declares that man "developed" morality through evolution is dumbfounding.

All of Psalm 119 is a guide for good living. It is a guide for understanding our vertical relationship with God as well as our horizontal relationship with our fellow men and women. Are there sacrifices to be made? Of course there are sacrifices to be made. Every good thing that you want to have or to be requires sacrifice. God's Word and His call to our being holy, or set apart, is not a straitjacket. His Word is our ultimate liberation. We become who we were meant to become.

That is living the "abundant life" that Jesus proclaimed. Jesus speaking in John 6:37-40 states, *"All that the Father gives me will come to me, and whoever comes to me I will never cast out. For I have come down from heaven, not to do my own will but the will of Him who sent me. And this is the will of Him who sent me, that I should lose nothing of all that He has given me, but raise it up on the last day. For this is the will of my Father, that everyone who looks on the Son and believes in Him should have eternal life, and I will raise him up on the last day."*

In contrast, you can read the classic book *Lord of the Flies* by William Golding. It highlights the fact that humans put in charge of their own godless ways will devolve into chaos and death rather than evolve (as the atheist believes) into a "cultured" society. That is man's true nature; that is our sinful nature. We'll look more at that in the chapters ahead.

And so, as we recognize our proper relationship with God and humble ourselves to our Creator in understanding that we are completely and forever dependent on Him, we set and reinforce the foundation to tell the world of our God.

Lesson 7 – From Doubt to Defense – Right Relationship

Verses: Genesis 1 – 2, Hebrews 11:6

Without a proper understanding of Who God is and who we are, it is impossible to form a correct defense of the Gospel. In this present day, Christians are truly running countercultural.

We need a foundational understanding of how we are to relate to God and how He relates to man.

Key Questions:

What does the Bible assert about God?

Is God revealing Himself today?

Creator vs. Creature

God's Independence –

Job 38 - 39

Man's Dependence –

1. Physical Dependence

Psalm 139:13–16

2. Historical Dependence

Romans 15:4, Acts 7

3. Knowledge

a. General revelation -
Psalm 19:1

b. Special revelation -
Hebrews 1:1–2 , John 6:44–51

4. Morality

Psalm 119

How would you sum up or put into perspective this Creator - Creature relationship to an unbeliever?

Copyright© Ronald Parrs 2025

Lesson 8 - The Sin Problem

There are many examples of "sin" throughout the Book of Acts. Commission, omission, word, deed, thought.

In Apologetics, we must deal with sin directly because sin directly interferes with our right Relationship with God.

As we look at Acts Chapter 7 (actually finishing up the last two paragraphs of Chapter 6), we see Stephen, a new leader in the Church, giving a great apologetic. It may look like a historical outline of Jewish history, but it's an apologetic nonetheless, especially as Stephen concludes.

In Chapter 7, we see a man, Stephen, a new Christian believer, being empowered by the Holy Spirit. Before his arrest, he did incredible things in the Name of God - healings, "signs and wonders." The local Jewish leaders couldn't argue against him. In the end, these men would "construct" accusations to smear Stephen to arrest him and ultimately remove him from the public (also hoping to put a major damper on this new "Jesus thing" by crushing the other followers' spirits). Instead, they saw in Stephen "the face of an angel" (Acts 6:15).

Most of the time we think of sin in bold and concrete terms: rape, murder, adultery, witchcraft, drunkenness, foul language, lying, cheating, and all of their "modes"—the usual crimes.

But then there are the sins we don't want to deal with. The little white lies; the cover-ups; the sins of omission - what we "forget" to do. After all, no one got hurt. What's a little porn watching? Your spouse won't find out - especially if you purge your laptop's history each time. Gambling is sometimes fun - except when the money was used for groceries or shared with someone who has nothing. Besides, you've gone to church and Sunday school and helped out at the local soup kitchen last month, not to mention you've had regular devotional times this week. We speak of the so-called "seven deadly sins" and don't realize that those sins are merely an outward manifestation of the inward reality of the sinfulness of our hearts and minds.

Oh, to return to the condition when we were first created! Man and woman without sin. Clean, fresh, knowing all that God wanted us to know. Thinking, speaking, and doing in perfect Godly wisdom and knowledge. We reasoned with God and used His logic, limited only by what God Himself placed upon our lives and minds. Some things were left to mystery, understanding that God was in control. We depended entirely on God's truth without hesitation. When you think about it, it's quite liberating.

And then came the Fall.

You see, I struggle too. Sin is insidious. Sin gets into every nook and cranny of our lives. It's a constant battle between the natural self and the life God wants you to lead. The battle of sin in our minds (memories, desires, lusts, biases, etc.) eventually bleeds out into our spoken words and, if left unchecked, leads to physical actions causing physical harm to other people, including those closest to us. It would probably be much easier to be a Christian and live in seclusion, but God wants us to live in this world. He wants us to be His ambassadors to a lost world. And so, He has us here, doing His work; rubbing elbows with those who need to know God.

These are the noetic effects of sin.

The "noetic" effects of sin are the effects of sin on the human mind and intellect; our moral problem leads to an intellectual problem. These are important, for as the mind goes, so goes the individual life. As we deny God and sin (in general and our individual sin problem), we push our minds toward sin and its consequences; in other words, the sin problem worsens.

Throughout Scripture, we see the noetic effects of sin. From the early chapters of Genesis, we see pride and arrogance in the Garden leading to Spiritual Death. Arrogance, stubbornness, and hardened hearts bring down kings and empires. Empty reasoning, from arrogance and a hardened heart, leads to a diminished understanding of Who God is and what He has and is doing in our lives. Ungodliness ending with a lack of care for any of God's creation, leading to a self-centered and self-destructive (at minimum in the sense of eternal separation from God) life.

Let's look at some Biblical examples of the noetic effects of sin: Psalm 10:2-11,

"In arrogance the wicked [further referred to as "he" or "his"] *hotly pursue the poor;*
   let them be caught in the schemes that they have devised.
For the wicked boasts of the desires of his soul,
   and the one greedy for gain curses and renounces the LORD.
In the pride of his face the wicked does not seek him;
   all his thoughts are, "There is no God."
His ways prosper at all times;
   your judgments are on high, out of his sight;
   as for all his foes, he puffs at them.
He says in his heart, "I shall not be moved;
   throughout all generations I shall not meet adversity."
His mouth is filled with cursing and deceit and oppression;
   under his tongue are mischief and iniquity.
He sits in ambush in the villages;
   in hiding places he murders the innocent.
His eyes stealthily watch for the helpless;
   he lurks in ambush like a lion in his thicket;
he lurks that he may seize the poor;
   he seizes the poor when he draws him into his net.
The helpless are crushed, sink down,
   and fall by his might.
He says in his heart, "God has forgotten,
   he has hidden his face, he will never see it."

Psalm 14:1, *"The fool says in his heart, 'There is no God.'*
They are corrupt, their deeds are vile; there is no one who does good."

Proverbs 26:4-5, *"Answer not a fool according to his folly, lest you be like him yourself. Answer a fool according to his folly, lest he be wise in his own eyes."* This is actually an effective apologetic strategy that we'll examine later in the study.

Proverbs 26:11, *"Like a dog returns to its vomit, is a fool who repeats his folly."*

Romans 1:18-20, *"For the wrath of God is revealed from heaven against all ungodliness and unrighteousness of men, who by their unrighteousness suppress the truth. For what can be known about God is plain to them, because God has shown it to them. For his invisible attributes, namely, his eternal power and divine nature, have been clearly perceived, ever since the creation of the world, in the things that have been made. So they are without excuse."*

Romans 8:7-8, *"For the mind that is set on the flesh is hostile to God, for it does not submit to God's law; indeed, <u>it cannot</u>. Those who are in the flesh cannot please God."* (emphasis mine).

This is all somewhat scary stuff to those of us who do believe and are right with God.

Ultimately, the arguments from the atheist or agnostic (polite atheists) are NOT intellectual arguments or intellectual issues. Deniers of God choose their lot; it is easier to deny God and their sin, rather than deal with their sin. Notice their arguments: "prostitution is a 'victimless' crime"; "adultery is between two consenting adults, so why not?"; "it's a woman's right to choose abortion"; "gay marriage is a 'right' for consenting adults".

So what does all this have to do Stephen's testimony before the Sanhedrin? After going through the History of the Jewish people, bringing attention to all that God had done, Stephen closes with the following words we read in Acts 7:51-53: *"You stiff-necked people, uncircumcised in heart and ears, you always resist the Holy Spirit. As your fathers did, so do you. Which of the prophets did your fathers not persecute? And they killed those who announced beforehand the coming of the Righteous One, whom you have now betrayed and murdered, you who received the law as delivered by angels and did not keep it."* Acts 7:51-53.

And with that, Stephen was taken out and stoned to death.

The rulers had the Law and the words of the prophets. They had all the Godly knowledge that they needed. They knew the times. Yet they resisted. Was it the power they preferred? Was it their pride? In the final days, these "holy" men had God Himself stand in their midst (in the person of Jesus Christ) to speak to them. But yet, their sin had completely blinded them to their own ruin.

And that's the rub of sin. At the time of sinning, it "feels" good. There's a certain pleasure to it. Regardless of how well we know or understand the sinfulness of the sin, to a degree, we still revel in it. When I think about that, it's disgusting. It's putrid. Why would I continue to sin? Why would I continue to go back to my own vomit?

I do these things - I sin - because that is my natural nature. In my foolishness, I always revert to my natural self; I return to sinning. And it takes effort to separate the sin from my life. In fact, the only way that I can separate sin from my life is to give place to it at the foot of the Cross and present it as sin for Jesus to take away. It is otherwise impossible for me to do anything about it. That is the pervasiveness of sin.

Paul says it best in Romans chapter 7:15-25, *"For I do not understand my own actions. For I do not do what I want, but I do the very thing I hate. Now if I do what I do not want, I agree with the law, that it is good. So now it is no longer I who do it, but sin that dwells within me. For I know that nothing good dwells in me, that is, in my flesh. For I have the desire to do what is right, but not the ability to carry it out. For I do not do the good I want, but the evil I do not want is what I keep on doing. Now if I do what I do not want, it is no longer I who do it, but sin that dwells within me.*

"So I find it to be a law that when I want to do right, evil lies close at hand. For I delight in the law of God, in my inner being, but I see in my members another law waging war against the law of my mind and making me captive to the law of sin that dwells in my members. Wretched man that I am! Who will deliver me from this body of death? Thanks be to God through Jesus Christ our Lord! So then, I myself serve the law of God with my mind, but with my flesh I serve the law of sin."

Paul, the great apostle and defender of the Faith, was a mess. But he knew the only way out of his misery. There was and is only one way: through Jesus Christ's sacrificial death and bodily resurrection. That's it; there's no other way. None.

How much more of a mess are we today living in a culture that is just as bad as it was 2000 years ago? We may think we are more sophisticated or cosmopolitan, but we are not really.

Even that idea is a lie. Are you - am I - willing to call ourselves "wretched" and throw ourselves on God's mercy? That's the only way out of this mess that sin wants to keep us in.

Like many today, the men doing the stoning were self-righteous. They believed themselves more moral or more "highly favored" than Stephen, even the man who stood to the side, holding their cloaks. But one day, God would reveal Himself to that man, too. Thankfully, he would realize his sin and do the right thing: repent and give his life to Christ.

When it's all said and done, our responsibility as a Christian believer is to cut through the folly of unbelief and the suppression of Truth by standing on the Word of God. The "natural" man chooses NOT to see God for who He is. Romans 1:18 - 19, and following through to verse 31, plainly shows that we "suppress" the truth. And it's a downward spiral from there. Eventually, God gives man (men and women) over to his own "self-inflicted" destruction.

There is a way out of this darkness and sin. The unbeliever needs to see their sin and their subsequent need for a personal Savior.

Lesson 8 – From Doubt to Defense – The Sin Problem

Verses: Acts 7, Psalm 10:2-11

Key Questions:

What is sin?
What are the "noetic" effects of sin?

Define Sin in your own words:

What was man like before the Fall?

Effects of Sin as it relates to:

God

Our Society

Culture in General

Our Personal Lives

The Noetic effects of Sin (look up Biblical references):

1. Stubbornness

2. Enmity against God

3. Seared conscience or hardened heart

4. Arrogance

5. Spiritual death

6. Foolishness

7. Empty reasoning or darkened understanding

8. Others?

How do the noetic effects of sin play into apologetics?

Dignity and Depravity

Christianity is the only religion or system or worldview that can explain both the dignity of man as well as the depravity of man.

"Then God said, 'Let us make man in our image, after our likeness. And let them have dominion over the fish of the sea and over the birds of the heavens and over the livestock and over all the earth and over every creeping thing that creeps on the earth.'

"So God created man in his own image,
  in the image of God he created him;
  male and female he created them.

"And God blessed them. And God said to them, 'Be fruitful and multiply and fill the earth and subdue it and have dominion over the fish of the sea and over the birds of the heavens and over every living thing that moves on the earth.'"

That's Genesis 1:26-28.

In Genesis chapter 2, we learn some specifics of how we were created. Keep in mind that everything in the created universe up to this point had been spoken into existence - the stars and planets, the plants and animals, angels and other heavenly beings. We humans were to be created in a very special and personal way, by the direct hand of God.

"...then the LORD God formed the man of dust from the ground and breathed into his nostrils the breath of life, and the man became a living creature.... The man gave names to all livestock and to the birds of the heavens and to every beast of the field. But for Adam there was not found a helper fit for him. So the LORD God caused a deep sleep to fall upon the man, and while he slept took one of his ribs and closed up its place with flesh. And the rib that the LORD God had taken from the man he made into a woman and brought her to the man." Genesis 2:7, 20-22.

Man and woman were created in the image of God.

We were created for a divine purpose. We were specially created. By breathing into man, God endowed us with many of His attributes because we are His image bearers. God expected man to rule over His creation: the earth and everything in it and on it. Our job was to tend to the earth. He commanded us to reproduce and populate the whole earth. We were to have dominion over it, but we were to be good stewards and use it properly according to God's will and purpose.

In these few short verses, God explains who we were supposed to be; who we were designed to be. God states that mankind, the human race, was divinely designed, formed and put into relationship. The relationship was to be horizontal and vertical. First, we were to be in right relationship with our Creator. We were to depend on Him for everything completely, which means everything, including the air we breathe. That's the vertical relationship.

Horizontally, we were to be in right relationship with our fellow human beings and the world around us. Our relationship was to "mimic" God's relationship within the Trinity.

In short, we were created divinely (although mankind is not, emphatically not, divine) and with dignity. We could stand tall, looking straight ahead and especially looking up to our Father. We were created perfectly just as God had desired. We were at our zenith. We could not "evolve" into anything higher. No, we would "devolve" into depravity.

But unlike the other sentient beings of His creation (angels and heavenly beings have free choice but cannot be redeemed), God gave us free will. He gave us the power to choose. We could choose to be in complete and perfect fellowship with God, ourselves, and the rest of creation, or not.

Looking back at Genesis 2, God only gave us one prohibition: not to eat from the tree of knowledge of good and evil. We could eat from any other tree in the Garden. That's all, just one prohibition. That should have been a pretty simple list to follow. Why didn't they eat from the Tree of Life is beyond me, but...

Then sin entered the world. Man fell. And he (and she) fell hard. All they had would now be turned against them, because of just one sin, one disobedient act. And that one disobedient act would instantly lead us into our depravity as a race. The good news is that our fall would not be irreversible, but we would fall. Fortunately, it wouldn't be a free-fall. Some part of us would recognize our sinful nature and hold us back from becoming utterly depraved.

In a short time, murder would creep in (Genesis 4:8-12). As time passed, mankind and demons would come together in an unholy alliance to produce depraved offspring (Genesis 6:1-5). And the depravity worsened. Even after the Flood, even after Noah and his family (righteous in God's eyes) personally witnessed God's wrath upon the earth, depravity snuck its ugly head in in the form of drunkenness and immodesty (Genesis 9:20-24).

And things only got worse. For centuries following, man's depravity would worsen. Despite our Creator making us for a relationship with Him, we can now become totally depraved by our choices. Look at our maximum-security prisons and cemeteries to see the results of our evil choices. Humanity's sin was now, and had been, a part of our fallen nature. Some babies die stillborn. Others don't survive abortion. No one has to teach a baby to cry, fuss, or feel uncomfortable, sick, scared, or lonely. Every toddler is now predisposed to throw a tantrum when disappointment sets in. While little ones remain innocent (before they truly know and understand right from wrong, humanity is no longer "naturally good." Innocent babies and toddlers grow into headstrong kids who can (and will) make their own evil choices. This is why we put children on "time-outs." They can't just blame Adam. Anyone who says children are "naturally good" has never raised a child or read the book of Proverbs.

As a parent, and especially as a dad, I can only keep directing them back to God. Even God, our heavenly Father, disciplines us, directing us back to His Word, and continues to teach us (them) how to renew our (their) hearts by renewing our (their) minds. That's something that I have to do continually. As Paul reminds us in Romans 12:1-2: *"I appeal to you therefore, brothers, by the mercies of God, to present your bodies as a living sacrifice, holy and acceptable to God, which is your spiritual worship. Do not be conformed to this world, but be transformed by the renewal of your mind, that by testing you may discern what is the will of God, what is good and acceptable and perfect."*

Definitions of Sin and Depravity.

Before we continue, we need to define the terms of Sin and Depravity. In the Old Testament, the Hebrew word "chata" (khata) is used to describe or define sin as "missing the mark" or "going astray" (Strong's Hebrew: 2398; Biblehub.com). Think of an archer with a bow and arrow aiming at a target, shooting, and hitting or missing the target. Did the arrow hit the target, accidentally miss the target (not aiming properly or a mis-shoot), or purposely miss the target? Another idea would be a person heading in a particular direction but intentionally or inadvertently "going astray." The "target" is God and His holiness and perfection; it's what He expects of men and women because we are created in His image and likeness. When we sin, either by commission (purposeful) or omission (laziness, forgetfulness, or "accidental"), we miss God's target for our lives. I'm going out on a limb to say that for the average person, our sin is minimal. We choose to see it (confession), correct it (repent), and aim again.

In creation, God has already made known to every man, woman, and child Who He is. Even to those who cannot read or have never heard the Gospel story, every human knows God through His creation. The beauty, the orderliness, the eternal laws of math, physics, chemistry, and even our humanness (love, joy, justice, mercy, anger) speak volumes about God and His nature. No one is without an excuse for knowing Him intimately and wanting a perfect and eternal relationship.

And then some people don't like the target. They don't want to live in God's universe of orderliness, love, justice, mercy, and grace – they want to create their version of Who God is. They desire a different target constructed in their image and likeness. Just take a look around, and you will see, and sometimes personally witness, the depravity of men and women. No one is immune to it. The American Heritage Dictionary (5th edition) defines depravity as "moral corruption or degradation" and "a vitiated [spoiled or corrupted] state of moral character; general badness of character; wickedness of mind or heart." We all participate in sin in one way or another, like it or not. We can't help but be sinful and, if left unchecked or unrepentant, become depraved.

"For all have sinned and fall short of the glory of God." Romans 3:23. Not some, not most, but ALL have sinned. That means everyone: you, me, our child, our spouse, our neighbor, our moms and dads, our pastors and priests, everyone.

None of us can hit the target—we all "miss the mark." Hopefully, we all want to hit the mark. Hopefully, we desire to be more godly and Christlike, which requires diligence. Bad habits are easy to get into; they're easy to commit and remain in. Good habits are difficult to maintain—good habits require self-discipline.

In Romans chapter one, the apostle Paul teaches us of the downward spiral when we continually "miss the mark" – when we continue to sin, by commission or omission. Paul is purposely forceful in this admonition because he understands the consequences of a sinful life and eventual eternal separation from God. We read, *"For the wrath of God is revealed from heaven against all ungodliness and unrighteousness of men, who by their unrighteousness suppress the truth. For what can be known about God is plain to them, because God has shown it to them. For his invisible attributes, namely, his eternal power and divine nature, have been clearly perceived, ever since the creation of the world, in the things that have been made. So they are without excuse. For although they knew God, they did not honor him as God or give thanks to him, but they became futile in their thinking, and their foolish hearts were darkened. Claiming to be wise, they became fools and exchanged the glory of the immortal God for images resembling mortal man and birds and animals and creeping things.*

"Therefore God gave them up in the lusts of their hearts to impurity, to the dishonoring of their bodies among themselves, because they exchanged the truth about God for a lie and worshiped and served the creature rather than the Creator, who is blessed forever! Amen.

"For this reason God gave them up to dishonorable passions. For their women exchanged natural relations for those that are contrary to nature; and the men likewise gave up natural relations with women and were consumed with passion for one another, men committing shameless acts with men and receiving in themselves the due penalty [consequences of sin] *for their error.*

"And since they did not see fit to acknowledge God, God gave them up to a debased mind to do what ought not to be done. They were filled with all manner of unrighteousness, evil, covetousness, malice. They are full of envy, murder, strife, deceit, maliciousness. They are gossips, slanderers, haters of God, insolent, haughty, boastful, inventors of evil, disobedient to parents, foolish, faithless, heartless, ruthless. Though they know God's righteous decree that those who practice such things deserve to die, they not only do them but give approval to those who practice them." Romans 1:18-32

There's much to unpack in this passage. We have forgotten who we are and Whose we are, and it starts by suppressing the truth. God eventually removes His hand of protection as we purposefully continue to live and enjoy our sins without confession or repentance. He allows us to fall further until our ultimate destruction or a realization that we need a Savior who is willing and able to save us.

Instead of rightly wearing the crown of God's glory that was prepared for us (please take a look at Job 19:8–10, Psalm 8, 103, Proverbs 4:1-9, Isaiah 62:1-5, and 1 Peter 5:4), we have put on the filth and debauchery of the world. We like it, and I would go so far as to say we even prefer sin. Our self-pride drags us down to the point where we are like that pig or dog, as we read in 2 Peter 2:17-22. As you read Romans chapters 1 and 2, you see how far the depravity would go, and it has gone. The Law of God and the Bible itself hold up a mirror to our faces to show us what we have chosen to become or act like.

Our depravity shows up in everything that we do. Our choices of television drama highlight man's depravity toward his fellow man and woman, whether it is sex, violence, or both. We allow the sins of abortion and sexual deviancy to flourish in our society with barely a peep of complaint. We get mad at the TV instead of getting out of our chairs and comfort zones and donning the righteousness given to us by God to combat the evil in the world. Most of the time, we don't even do it in our own lives.

One of my favorite genres of television drama is crime or criminal drama. Two of my "favorite" shows are *"Criminal Minds"* and *"Law & Order: Criminal Intent"*. What I "like" about them is that they expose man's true heart and mind. Man's total depravity and his (or her) intentions and actions toward our fellow humans are typically less than altruistic. It is much easier to sin against someone than to aid, edify, or lift another person. We have to work at being and acting "good."

The other thing that I "like" about these two programs is that they display the noetic effects of sin. The noetic effects of sin are the effects that affect the mind—and, ultimately, the effects of our relationship with God. Too many times, I've turned off an episode, and I feel like I need a mental shower. Instead of being in God's Word on a daily basis to purge and cleanse our minds, we often don't, and we forget who we are.

Redemption is available.

Even though God reveals Himself throughout nature, history, and His Word, we had and have a choice. But we more often than not choose depravity over divine dignity. And to make matters worse, we would even choose to make God in our image if possible. Oh, how far we have fallen.

The good news is that God provided, and still provides, a way (one way) of Redemption to right the broken relationship. From the beginning, the Bible teaches - and explicitly states - that God came looking for man. The man was hiding from God. Adam and Eve knew they had sinned and wanted to hide from God. That act is genuinely laughable. How do you hide from God? At least when God caught up with them, they were relatively honest about what had happened. But notice the buck-passing that ensues: *"Now the serpent was more crafty than any other beast of the field that the Lord God had made.*

"He said to the woman, 'Did God actually say, 'You shall not eat of any tree in the garden'?' And the woman said to the serpent, 'We may eat of the fruit of the trees in the garden, but God said, 'You shall not eat of the fruit of the tree that is in the midst of the garden, neither shall you touch it, lest you die.'' But the serpent said to the woman, 'You will not surely die. For God knows that when you eat of it your eyes will be opened, and you will be like God, knowing good and evil.' So when the woman saw that the tree was good for food, and that it was a delight to the eyes, and that the tree was to be desired to make one wise, she took of its fruit and ate, and she also gave some to her husband who was with her, and he ate. Then the eyes

of both were opened, and they knew that they were naked. And they sewed fig leaves together and made themselves loincloths.

"And they heard the sound of the Lord God walking in the Garden in the cool of the day, and the man and his wife hid themselves from the presence of the Lord God among the trees of the Garden. But the Lord God called to the man and said to him, 'Where are you?' And he [Adam] *said, 'I heard the sound of you in the garden, and I was afraid, because I was naked, and I hid myself.' He* [God] *said, 'Who told you that you were naked? Have you eaten of the tree of which I commanded you not to eat?' The man said, 'The woman whom you gave to be with me, she gave me fruit of the tree, and I ate.' Then the Lord God said to the woman, 'What is this that you have done?' The woman said, 'The serpent deceived me, and I ate.'* Genesis 3:1-13.

This could be the end, but we're just getting started.

Now, back to the unfolding redemption story.

God always wants to redeem His creation. He loved - and loves - His creation. He loved - and loves - His image bearers. And He would do everything He possibly could to make that happen. From the foundations of the world, God chose to restore the divine dignity He had originally bestowed on us. There would be a process. It would take His timing. God Himself would put every event in history in motion to make that happen. He would start His redemption process right there in the Garden. God made the first blood sacrifice to atone for the sins of the first couple (Genesis 3:21).

Over the following millennia, the Trinity—Father, Son, and Holy Spirit—worked tirelessly to redeem their creation. From time to time, they punctuated history and were with Abraham, Moses, or Daniel. God spoke through His prophets, telling His people what to expect, always calling us back to holiness and to a personal relationship with Him.

Finally, Jesus would come and provide the sacrifice that would end all others. For over thirty years, God would walk and talk freely among us in the Person of Jesus. After His Resurrection and Ascension, the Holy Spirit was sent to dwell in anyone who would accept His sacrificial atonement and believe in this finished work of the Cross.

With the sealing of the Holy Spirit, our dignity and relationship with God are restored. The loss mankind suffered in the Garden was not complete; it was temporary. A few thousand years is temporary in God's scheme of things.

The uniqueness of Christianity.

You won't find this explanation of dignity and depravity in any other belief, philosophical, or religious system. We can only grasp our proper place in God's Creation in the Bible. Only in and by Christ are we restored. Created in and with dignity, we fell into depravity due to our own choice, our own choices. That's where the story ends in every other religion or belief system. From there, you scramble to work for your salvation. You foolishly and fruitlessly keep reaching up, trying to do "good" and be "good enough" for God to accept you.

But there's only ONE thing you can do: submit yourself, put yourself in God's loving hands, and accept His will and means of salvation. With His forgiveness and the indwelling of the Holy Spirit, you can have your dignity restored. Will you fight your sin and depravity? Yes. But because of God, the fight is over. God has won.

If you've never trusted Jesus Christ as your personal Savior, would you do it now? You can never be good enough on your own, but God wants to restore you by the Holy Spirit. If you are genuinely sorry for your sinfulness and want God to save you and bring you to eternal life, I would ask you to say this simple prayer of forgiveness and repentance.

Here's how to pray: Say it aloud so you can hear it; God already knows your heart. Let me help you.

Dear God, I have done many bad and evil things. I want to clean up my life, but I can't do it with my own power. I need your love and help. You've said in the Bible that if I confess my sins, You are faithful and will take away my sins and purify me. Lord, take away my sins and purify me. I recognize that only the death of Jesus can do this. I know I am guaranteed eternal life with you by Jesus' Resurrection. I accept this free gift from you. Thank you for being my God and Savior. Amen.

Take seriously what you have prayed. If you need someone to come alongside you to help you on your way, ask God to direct you to the right person. Ask God to direct you to a good Bible-believing and teaching church. Pray. Read the Bible. Ask the Holy Spirit to explain what you're reading. He will teach you.

Lesson 9 - The Redemption Solution

All of us live in "good news and bad news" tension. Following good news, there is often times bad news and vice versa. Now it may not happen immediately, but the opposite will occur in due time.

As we just discussed, the problem of sin is the problem of the ages. Sin separates us from our dependency upon God. Sin breaks the Creator-creature relationship.

And remember that it's not just what we do, the real roots of sin are in the mind and in the intellect. As our thoughts go, so go our behaviors and attitudes. Those who choose to ignore or push God to the side, along with sin, can continue sinning all the day long. And since their mindset is nihilistic (there is nothing and whatever we see and experience came out of chaos as opposed to a Created, purposeful creation), they believe they have nothing to worry about.

The Truths of Sin and Redemption.

For the believing Christian, we have the hope and reality of Redemption. As we have heard the Gospel of God revealed through general revelation in the world around us, and through Special Revelation, Holy Scripture, we see God continually reaching out to His creation desiring to restore that original relationship. First, we hear, then through the power of the Holy Spirit, we are able to believe. And just because we have chosen to believe and accept God's invitation, God redeems and saves us. Do you understand the power of that?

The truth of the Gospel is that no matter how bad my sin is - and if you believe or think that I'm a no-good, good-for-nothing, well, you don't even know the half of it. And by the way, you had better look at your life too. God's standard is perfection, and none of us, not one, is perfect. We - that means you and I, regardless of who you are - are sinful, putrid messes and enemies of God. To make matters worse, we can do nothing about it on our own or by our own power.

How does that make you feel? Lousy? Don't worry, there truly is good news: God's Good News. God's Gospel.

For the Christian, it's bad news - by sin we are fallen and separated from God - followed by good news (Gospel means good news) - by God's power, not our own, we are redeemed and restored to a dependent Creator-creature relationship. Whatever we need, want, desire, or hope for, we rely on God alone. In fact, when we are at our lowest, when we are at our weakest, God is most able to do and to provide. We humans have virtually no power compared to God, Who is all-powerful.

For the unbelieving man or woman, they are in a bad news-bad news scenario. They are separated from God as soon as they can think and process ideas. They purposefully and continually push God away: His creation, His Words (through the written Word or the spoken word of believers), and especially the Holy Spirit (as we progress further in the study, I'll share a quote from Jean Paul Sartre). That's why the apostle Paul states in Romans 12:2 that the redemption and transformation process begins by renewing our minds, enabling us to know God and His purposes and will for our lives. Let's read it again: *"Do not be conformed to this world, but be transformed by the renewal of your mind, that by testing you may discern what is the will of God, what is good and acceptable and perfect."* Without redemption, the individual is lost forever.

But there really is good news for anybody reading this study who has never understood how much God loves you. You see, as awful and sinful as you and I are, God loves us even more! In fact, He loves us so much that He sent His Son, His only Son, to die and pay the penalty for sin in your place. How great is that?

Here's how it works...

In order to be Restored, we are Redeemed by Regeneration. Jesus Himself has told us that we must be "born again". That famous verse that you hear and see all over the place is John 3:16 and following through to verse 18. Here it is: *"For God so loved the world, that he gave his only Son, that whoever believes in him should not perish but have eternal life. For God did not send his Son into the world to condemn the world, but in order that the world might be saved through him. Whoever believes in him is not condemned, but whoever does not believe is condemned already, because he has not believed in the name of the only Son of God."*

By believing we live. When we refuse to believe, by faith alone, we die. A couple of verses before that, Jesus says that it is only by the Spirit from above that we can be born again, *"That which is born of the flesh is flesh, and that which is born of the Spirit is spirit."* John 3:6

Furthermore, when we are regenerated, we become "new creations*", "Therefore, if anyone is in Christ, he is a new creation. The old has passed away; behold, the new has come. All this is from God, who through Christ reconciled us to himself and gave us the ministry of reconciliation; that is, in Christ God was reconciling the world to himself, not counting their trespasses against them, and entrusting to us the message of reconciliation."* 2 Corinthians 5:17-19

We are made new and are now reconciled to God.

I don't know about you, but I think this is really Good News! In fact it's GREAT News. In double fact, it even gets better if you will believe it...

Our entire being is made new and restored to the way God intended. We are restored to His likeness. Ephesians 4:23-24 states that we are *"...to be renewed in the spirit of your minds, and to put on the new self, created after the likeness of God in true righteousness and holiness."*

Paul further writes in Colossians 3:9-10, *"seeing that you have put off the old self with its practices and have put on the new self, which is being renewed in knowledge after the image of its Creator."*

As we allow the Spirit of God to transform us, as it were, from the inside out, we actually desire to bear fruit for Him. We want God to be glorified by work in and through presenting good works to the world around us. The trials and tribulations of this life may become difficult (even unto death or persecution). Still, because the Creator-creature relationship has been restored, we are confident in our dependence on God.

This is tremendous News! If you don't believe what I've just told you, open a Bible and read these verses in their full context. You'll see for yourself.

Being dependent on Someone, especially God, is a very good thing. There is nothing wrong with being dependent on the Creator of the Universe. And because He loves you as much as He does, He's willing to chase you down, die for you, and then live for you.

The finished work of Jesus at the cross not only took away all of the sin of the entire world for all time, past and future, but also provided the gateway to approach God. Jesus, as fully God and fully man, was the only One who could provide the sacrifice that would satisfy and restore the broken relationship. The sinful man can now approach the throne of Grace to receive mercy. The writer of the book of Hebrews states in chapter 4:16, *"Let us then with confidence draw near to the throne of grace, that we may receive mercy and find grace to help in time of need."*

Yes, we can confidently approach God for grace and mercy anytime. He is willing and He is able to save you from anything, even yourself.

But Redemption is just the beginning. The sanctification process is a lifelong process. Since we are still flesh and blood, we still struggle with our sinful nature. Will we continue to sin? Of course, but the indwelling of the Spirit of God also continues to prick our consciences and redirect our paths back toward God and His holiness. We want to do what is right and holy, but oftentimes we simply can't. Even Paul struggled and called himself "wretched," and so we cling even tighter to God, our Creator. We've looked at Romans 7:23 - 8:11, in part before, but it's worth revisiting as we close this chapter; it reads, *"...but I see in my members another law waging war against the law of my mind and making me captive to the law of sin that dwells in my members. Wretched man that I am! Who will deliver me from this body of death? Thanks be to God through Jesus Christ our Lord! So then, I myself serve the law of God with my mind, but with my flesh I serve the law of sin.*

"There is therefore now no condemnation for those who are in Christ Jesus. For the law of the Spirit of life has set you free in Christ Jesus from the law of sin and death. For God has done what the law, weakened by the flesh, could not do. By sending his own Son in the likeness of sinful flesh and for sin, he condemned sin in the flesh, in order that the righteous requirement of the law might be fulfilled in us, who walk not according to the flesh but according to the

Spirit. For those who live according to the flesh set their minds on the things of the flesh, but those who live according to the Spirit set their minds on the things of the Spirit. For to set the mind on the flesh is death, but to set the mind on the Spirit is life and peace. For the mind that is set on the flesh is hostile to God, for it does not submit to God's law; indeed, it cannot. Those who are in the flesh cannot please God.

"You, however, are not in the flesh but in the Spirit, if in fact the Spirit of God dwells in you. Anyone who does not have the Spirit of Christ does not belong to him. But if Christ is in you, although the body is dead because of sin, the Spirit is life because of righteousness. If the Spirit of him who raised Jesus from the dead dwells in you, he who raised Christ Jesus from the dead will also give life to your mortal bodies through his Spirit who dwells in you."

That's really good news. Those are also great passages to read and re-read again and again. Reading God's Word is like a "mental shower" in this world of continual bombardment in sight and sound of all of this world's "news". We need to be cleansed from the inside out. Living this life is a regular, daily struggle. Many do not want you to succeed.

Yet as the world around us watches our struggle, they are sometimes amazed.

Today the idea of "spirituality" or being a "spiritual person" provides us with both a problem as well as an opportunity. The problem is that many have an idea of who God is, but it's not the God of the Bible. Their idea can be this "unseen Force of the Universe" but it is not the Tri-unity of Father, Son and Holy Spirit that we know and love.

And here is the opportunity: to be able to testify as to what God has done in our own personal lives. We are able to go beyond "knowing about God" and to explain (present an apologia) the relationship that we have, and that is available to them, to the Living God who made them. Just as we read of "spiritual people" in Acts chapter 8 - Simon the sorcerer and the Ethiopian eunuch, they needed to hear the Truth of the Gospel. They needed to have someone who knew God and His Word, reveal and help explain it. Go and read those amazing stories. Simple, everyday people, like you and me who are obedient in sharing God's Word and God's Truth with others who are seeking and need an encouraging human word, powered by the Holy Spirit.

We are not to remain silent. We are to be prepared and be bold in our witness, presenting the Truth and Hope that resides in each of our lives.

Lesson 9 – From Doubt to Defense – The Redemption Solution

Verses: Romans 12:1-2, Acts 8

Key Questions:

What is redemption?
Why does redemption begin in the mind?

Define Redemption in your own words:

What is the Redemption process?

Reversing the Fall:

How

The Effects

Restoration by Regeneration:

How

The Effects

The Responsibilities

Redemption vs. Sanctification

Why?

What about Spirituality?

Lesson 10 - A Christian Worldview, part 1

Back in the 1970s, comedian Bill Cosby had a routine featuring Noah and God. God divinely revealed materials and dimensions to Noah, telling him how to build the ark. Finally, Noah responded, " What's a cubit?"

Without knowing what a cubit is, how could he build the ark to the proper dimensions that God required for the survival of mankind and the animal kingdom?

As we begin discussing "worldviews," we must first define what a "Worldview" is. Essentially, a worldview is how an individual looks at the world around him or her. How that person looks at the world around them is determined or defined by an individual's personal attitudes, philosophy, background, and upbringing. We view life and interpret life through the lens of our worldview.

The fact of the matter is that EVERYONE has a worldview. No matter who you are or where you live, you have a worldview. You know how the world looks or operates according to your beliefs. For example, a top-level executive living on the 49th floor of a swanky East Side Manhattan condo *can* have a much different worldview than a tribal chieftain in western Kenya, a thriving fisherman in Hong Kong, or a teenager in Rio de Janeiro. Each has a different background, upbringing, and socio-economic setting. Never mind religious views and values, language, customs, and more. And each of these factors helps to shape and determine a person's worldview.

Not to belabor the point, but even two students living next door to each other in suburban America can have differing worldviews. One is male, the other female. One has a stay-at-home mom; the other has a mom who works the second shift. One is of a Catholic background and attends Mass every week; the other wants to go to church with another friend, but the parents don't allow it because they believe the "child" should make their own decisions when they are older. One helps in a local soup kitchen every month; the other won't lift a finger around the house. Their worldviews color how they think about the world around them and how they participate in society.

Young or old, rich or poor, black or white, Protestant or Buddhist—you plug in the variables—everyone has a worldview. And worldviews *can* change. Ideas and thinking can change a person, and life's crises can change a worldview.

A change of mind.

Look at Acts chapter 9, which is a fantastic, supernatural example of a change in someone's worldview. Saul, a student of the great Jewish rabbi Gamaliel, a persecutor of this new "religion" or sect who calls themselves "Christians" or followers of "the Way," changes his worldview. Saul becomes Paul. By the power of the Holy Spirit, he now sees the world as God sees it. Before his conversion, Saul saw the world through one set of lenses. Yes, it may have been in the Jewish tradition and close to God, but it was still out of focus. Saul was a "Pharisee" and therefore believed in an eventual resurrection as opposed to being a "Sadducee" who would not have believed in a resurrection. God needed to remove the scales from his eyes so that he could see everything the way God did. And that means everything.

When we see with "new" eyes, we have a change of mind. We renew our minds, and as our minds are renewed, everything else changes.

Some people may argue that it is first a change of heart. That may be close, but God uses a change of mind first. God wants us to reason this all out. The heart is full of feelings, and He has already said that our hearts are *"deceitful above all things."* Jeremiah 17:9. God wants us to think. He wants us to use our minds. It's not that we are to forsake our emotions, but our emotions can very well mislead us and point or direct us away from the Truth and even God. When in balance, the mind and heart temper one another.

Why is understanding worldviews important to the study and participation of Apologetics? Without understanding the other party's worldview, we don't know how they think or what "makes them tick," as Sigmund Freud put it. Furthermore, we need to be able to communicate our Christian Trinitarian (explained below) worldview to them rather than just argue for a "Supreme Sentient Being" devoid of personality or relationship. This is the idea of "Christian Theism." In the following chapters, we'll overview general non-Christian worldviews.

In his book, "The Universe Next Door," James Sire (Intervarsity Press, 5th edition, 2009) develops the idea that seven parts or questions come into play as we construct our worldview.

As we go through these questions, I'll plug in the Evangelical Christian (this is going to be a broad brush approach, so beware and please allow me some leeway) ideas that go along and support these worldviews. In determining a worldview (yours or another person's), we essentially ask: "What is the Nature of..." And so, let's begin.

The first question we ask is, "What is the Nature of Reality?" The philosophical term would be understanding the metaphysical or Ontological. What is really real? Is there a god? If there is, what does he, she, or it look like or act like? No matter what, when defining a person's worldview, we must define God (Theology) or the absence of Him. And what of our being?

In defending the Christian Faith (orthodox, Bible-believing, fundamental), our Ontology and Theology is that God does exist, and He exists in the "form" of 3 Persons: Father, Son, and Holy Spirit. These Persons make up the Godhead. God is Triune in Nature. The Father is God, Jesus Christ is God, and the Holy Spirit is God. Without this doctrine firmly in place, our apologetic is crushed. We don't even know Who God is. How, then, do we accurately and positively present our apologetic to an atheist or, agnostic or Eastern religious (Buddhist, Hindu, Shinto, etc.) person? What about that "spiritual" friend who is constantly looking here and there for a "blessed" time of refreshment? That person is as lost as the atheist! Remember that getting "close" doesn't count in God's economy. You're either Saved or lost, Redeemed or unregenerate. God has no middle ground.

As Christians, we naturally believe in the "supernatural." That is, we believe that there exists something or a 'realm' beyond what our senses can determine. Our reality is the unseen, the seen, the invisible, and the visible. That is part of our creed.

The second question asks, "What is the Nature of the world around us?" What is our Cosmology? Not just the ground under our feet but the planet(s), the creatures inhabiting it, the solar system, and beyond. Where did it all come from? Where is it all going? How is it constructed?

The studies and our understanding of biology, geology, physics, chemistry, and astronomy come from Cosmology. We debate Creationism versus evolution. We seemingly split hairs over "old earth" versus "new earth." The Bible, as a book of Natural Observation, states that the earth, the universe, and all that we see or don't see (the microscopic world as well as the universe beyond what we can observe) were created by God in six literal twenty-four-hour days, as the Bible states. Some theologians and others translate the days into epochs or eons to better support their worldview; after all, evolution needs time, and the more time, the better to make it all fit.

I rely on the Bible as God's True Word as a Christian. I can't pick and choose what I agree with or don't. It's either 100% true or it's not. If there is even ONE error in the Bible, then God has lied, and the entire volume is false. And so, by Faith, I believe that God created all that I see and experience in six literal twenty-four-hour days and then rested on the seventh day. It is far easier to believe and accept Divine Creation rather than go through all of the mental gymnastics of evolution.

Creationism is a simple and plausible "theory." Let's face it: no one, I repeat, no one was there in the beginning to see it all happen except God. For the Christian who believes in evolution (which is its own "faith" or "religion"), I ask the question: if you don't believe (have Faith) in six literal days of Creation, then what do you do with Revelation chapters 21 and 22? How many billions of years will God need to make the new Heavens, Earth, and Jerusalem happen? Remember that God is constant, consistent, and immutable in all He does.

And since we're talking about Creation, what of God's pinnacle of Creation, humanity?

Our third question: What is the Nature of man? What is our Anthropology? Where did we come from? What about gender? Why do men differ from women? Why do women want the seat down on a toilet? How can men be thinking of nothing? What happens after we die?

Christians believe God created humanity (one race) in two forms: male and female. They have different bodies and functions, but both are created in God's image. Eve was taken from Adam and specially formed as a helpmate for him. God knew that man needed a woman. Knowing and believing you are created in God's image gives you purpose. You have worth and dignity.

The child that a woman is carrying as she is pregnant is not a "bundle of tissue." From the moment of conception, the DNA from the mom and dad is combined to create a brand new, unique human being. This baby, when born, will not only have unique (one-of-a-kind in the entire universe) DNA, but also fingerprints, brain waves, speech patterns, and other peculiarities. Even if there were twins or triplets or more, each baby is a unique creation. How can that be?

For the above reasons, most Christians are so utterly pro-life and pro-heterosexual marriage. Gay marriage is, according to God, an abomination in His sight. God created men, men, and women, women. He didn't mess up the genders. God created us for procreation and mutual enjoyment. Two men cannot conceive and give birth to a baby; neither can two women. For a baby to happen, the egg needs the sperm as much as the sperm needs the egg. Conception is impossible otherwise. One sex needs the other. The sexes complement and complete each other. More importantly, God wants this homosexual man or woman to realize their sin and error and return to Him. He wants that out of pure Love.

At our death, the Christian believes that the soul, being reunited with its resurrected body, will either spend eternity enjoying God in Heaven or endure a lonely, eternal hell of punishment and damnation. People have had chances over their entire lives to see, comprehend, and receive God as their personal Savior and Lord. Those who accept the Sovereignty and excellence of God live eternally. Those who ignore or choose not to believe die eternally. Like it or not, this proposition is "fair" because it's God's universe, and we exist under His rules. If you still have a problem with that, review lessons 5, 6, and 7 of this study.

Sociology, psychology, and cultural studies also fall under anthropology. What do we believe about an afterlife? That can be a sub-category or a criterion. The last question of Teleology, found in part 2 of this Christian worldview series, also deals with this question.

Is that enough to think about for a little while? Thought so! Let's digest this before moving on to part 2.

A Christian Worldview, part 2

As we discover our basic beliefs, we can construct our "personal" worldview.

As we have already discussed, James Sire's book The Universe Next Door contains seven (or eight, depending on how you want to group them) criteria that contribute to your worldview.

We briefly examined Ontology, the nature of reality; cosmology, the nature of the universe and the world around us; and Anthropology, the nature of man.

These lay the foundation for constructing a personal worldview. But those philosophies and ideas aren't the only criteria that define our worldview. Let's look at the remaining four.

The fourth criterion to examine is the Nature of Knowledge or Epistemology. In other words, how do you know what you know? On what do you base your assumptions? What or who is your Authority? What is your basis for believing (fill in the blank) to be true?

When it comes to the orthodox, Bible-believing Christian, there is only One Authority on which to base our knowledge and assumptions. That Authority is God and His Word (they are one and the same). The saying, "God said it, I believe it, that settles it," may sound trite, but it's true. Christians rely on God to be Truthful all of the time. If He weren't, He wouldn't be God. His nature is Holy and True, as well as immutable. He can't and doesn't change Himself to suit a changing fancy. If He did change, He would cease to be God.

Whether it be scientific knowledge of the weather, the movement of the planets, or the growth of a child in its mother's womb, God's Word speaks forthrightly and correctly. The wording may not be satisfactory, technical, or "scientific," but the ideas, wisdom, and knowledge are understandable and truthful by almost anyone. Is poetic license used in Scripture to describe specific astronomical observations? Of course, the book of Psalms is, after all, a book of Poetry. Even in common parlance, we say that the sun rises and sets. A proper observation notes that the sun is "stationary" while the Earth rotates and revolves around the sun.

The believing Christian acknowledges God as the ultimate source of all knowledge and wisdom. We can rest assured of those facts. I believe in a literal six-day period of Creation because I trust God as my ultimate source of Authority and truth. Science and information change, but God does not. Since I believe that God designed and created all, I can trust Him to provide dependable facts. I may use scientific methods to confirm Biblical observations, but God is proven correct. Is faith involved? Of course. But to believe the theory of evolution, you have to have faith, and maybe even more.

Observing the universe, we see incredible and infinite order in everything. Not one molecule or atom is out of place. We can not only observe the laws of science (gravity, entropy, thermodynamics, motion, etc.) and mathematics (algebra, geometry, calculus, 1+1 will always equal two or the square root of 25 will always be 5, we can calculate the area of a circle with a precise equation, etc.) Einstein's theory of relativity will always be $E=mc^2$. Light will always travel at 186,000 miles (300,000 kilometers) per second.

All of this order could not have come out of chaos. We have never observed or witnessed anything to become more orderly from disorder (for proof, look at your bathroom or teenager's bedroom), even given "sufficient" time (how many more billions of years might be needed?). To believe that order can proceed from disorder demands incredible faith. This orderliness and design require a Designer.

Fifth, what is the Nature of Morality? What about Ethics? Today, our society and the culture around us are in turmoil, in my opinion (and probably the opinion of many others), due to the degradation of morals and morality. At both the societal and personal levels, morals are crumbling. How many people do you know who say (or believe) the statement, "What's true for you isn't necessarily true for me?". Relative morality is not a modern problem. It is a centuries-old dilemma. Remember what Pontius Pilate asked Jesus in his inquisition: "What is Truth?" (John 18:38). Pilate was looking for something, anything by which he could either properly condemn Jesus or set Him free.

Christians can rely 100% on God for truth and absolutes. We have confidence that because God is Truth, He can only reveal truth. It is God who sets the Standards. God is the Nature of Truth. Out of truth come Morality and Ethics. God has given us a sense of right and wrong and clear laws and rules. There are laws of physics, but even those laws cannot ignore the truth. The first and second laws of thermodynamics should easily align science with God, but we'll consider this in the future. Furthermore, because we are image bearers of God himself, we have an ingrained conscience; we know the difference between good and evil.

This conscience (spirit) or morality belongs to man alone. Animals don't possess it. Yes, they may seem kind or vicious. Certain animals may kill other animals, but it is out of instinct or survival. The animals protect their young and feed their families. They do not kill without malice or forethought (except to feed). Man "instinctively" knows right from wrong and, depending on his or her moral state, chooses to follow either of those two paths, sometimes even crossing back and forth between them, to satisfy himself or herself. Even the born-again, redeemed Christian, saved from his sins, struggles with these morals and temptations. For this reason, the apostle Paul writes, *"For I do not understand my own actions. For I do not do what I want, but I do the very thing I hate."* (Romans 7:15).

Here are several simple examples to make the point: the non-Christian or even atheist knows that when he sees a child being bullied at the playground or witnesses a blatantly bad sports call, he knows that it's just plain wrong, and he's indignant. The opposite is also true: we smile as we watch a young preschooler help their playground buddy get up after tumbling off the slide and comfort them. We know right motives and a sense of morality spur those actions. Morality and ethics are "pre-programmed" into man's mind by a Holy God. That's His gift to us.

Our sixth question is the question of Teleology. What is the Nature of Life's Purpose? Does your life have an ultimate purpose? What is our Purpose? Why do we get up in the morning? Why do we work? Why do we educate ourselves and others? Why do we seek direction for our lives? Is there a purpose to History?

Some people think that the book of Ecclesiastes ("Meaningless, meaningless." Ecclesiastes 1:1) is a Biblical call for a belief in meaninglessness (and therefore a belief in nihilism - "nothingness"). No! Nothing could be further from the truth. Ecclesiastes is a call for complete reliance upon God for meaning and purpose. He alone provides us with purpose and a whole and abundant life. When we do anything apart from God, it may be meaningless, but performing any task or function with the idea of bringing glory to God (using the talents and desires given to us) provides absolute purpose.

Rhetorically, we can ask the question(s): Why did this happen to me? What would have happened if that person weren't around then? (Choose any historical moment with a specific person who appeared to "change" the destiny of a nation or even a family.

Here's a biblical example: the Jewish people were about to be exterminated because of an edict that was promulgated under false pretexts by King Ahasuerus (Xerxes, an actual historical figure). The plot to undo this edict required someone inside the palace who could help uncover the details, and so it fell to the young Hebrew maiden Esther. At first, she was stunned and unsure of how she could make a difference in saving her people. Her uncle Mordecai speaks to Esther, saying, *"Do not think to yourself that in the king's palace you will escape any more than all the other Jews. For if you keep silent at this time, relief and deliverance will rise for the Jews from another place, but you and your father's house will perish. And who knows whether you have not come to the kingdom for such a time as this?"* Esther 4:13-14

For such a time as this... Have you ever wondered why you were born in your particular birthplace to your particular parents and at this particular time in History? It is not an accident. Each of us is here (geographically and temporally) for a specific purpose. Every one of us has purpose; not just a purpose, but purpose. This is yet another aspect of God's orderliness.

As Christians, we see nature around us with different eyes. We recognize the beauty and complexity of the workmanship of God wherever we look. We find purpose in getting up in the morning and going to school or work. We find meaning in developing personal relationships; others enrich our lives. We exult in corporate worship of God with other believers (hopefully regardless of ethnicity or culture). Sunday mornings are not a waste of time. Being on a beautiful golf course for a nine o'clock tee time is not communing with God. Sunday mornings and other times spent studying God's Word restores and recharges our souls and beings so that we are better prepared to minister to the world in which God has placed us. Even study times should be considered times of worship and praise.

Finally, there is the question of Commitment. There's no "ology" here. Our worldview is ultimately a matter of the heart. We ask ourselves as we think, live, and relate, "Am I committed to..." This is deeper than a sense of purpose as just discussed. The idea of Commitment strikes at our core values.

When faced with adversity or differing opinions on worldviews, what will we do as individuals? Will we put a stake in the ground and stay committed to these core beliefs, or will we be swayed by cunning words or ideas? Will we buckle under the pressure to conform?

How committed are you to… your work? How about your spouse? How committed are you to your children and the family? Some of us, especially men, are so committed to our job or profession that we are willing to sacrifice our family to excel, while, of course, saying that we're doing it for the ultimate benefit of our family. I am guilty as charged.

But what of our Commitment to something even more extraordinary and also eternal? The question that I ask myself is this: how committed am I to God and His plans and His purposes? And perhaps furthermore, how committed am I to be used by God as He works in me and through me for those plans and purposes?

Sometimes it isn't easy to look into the mirror and ponder those essential questions.

As we have traveled this road of Christian Apologetics and a defense of Christian Theism, we return to that question of conformity. It is the question of the mind. Let's look at Romans 12:1-2 again: *"I appeal to you therefore, brothers, by the mercies of God, to present your bodies as a living sacrifice, holy and acceptable to God, which is your spiritual worship. Do not be conformed to this world, but be transformed by the renewal of your mind, that by testing you may discern what is the will of God, what is good and acceptable and perfect."*

True Christianity is not only counter-cultural; it is a paradigm shift in thinking. Even more, it is life and world-changing. By God's Grace, we can see the world, people, and all of Creation through His eyes. When we do that, we can work as His hands, feet, ears, and mouth in transforming this world and restoring it to the way God meant it. We "cross the aisle" not to compromise but to bring the unbelieving world to see and understand God's point of view. We maintain our stake in the ground.

Good works are done for God's Glory and set people free to be who God created them to be. The missionary in the jungles (natural or manmade) is there to tell people the Good News of God to save them for eternity and lift them out of ignorance and poverty (funny how those two scourges go together with an unbelieving world). People are truly liberated when they are exposed to the truth of who they are and in whose image they are created.

Will we succeed in this endeavor? Bluntly, no, not in our own strength and knowledge. Only God will succeed. In the end, it is God who finally redeems, restores, and regenerates His Creation. We are called to follow Him, share His story, and provide *"a reason for the Hope that we have"* within us. (1 Peter 3:15). That's enough work.

What is my personal worldview? That follows next...

Lesson 10 – From Doubt to Defense – The Christian Worldview

Verses: Romans 12:1-2, Acts 9

Key Questions:

What is a worldview?
Can a person's worldview change or be changed?

Facts are interpreted by our worldview.

A person's Worldview is made of how we view the world around us. We look at the world around us by answering the questions: "What is the Nature of…"

1. Ontology

2. Cosmology

3. Anthropology

4. Epistemology

5. Ethics

6. Teleology

7. Commitment

How did Paul's Worldview change?

What is your worldview?

Has your worldview changed?

How would you express your worldview to a "seeker"?

A Worldview Example

I was raised in a business-owning family in middle-class America in the late 20th Century. I attended church and public school and could travel and live abroad. So, what is my worldview?

That's a fair question. The above items have contributed to how my worldview has been constructed. As you've been reading, you probably have a pretty good idea of what it is. But let's go beyond and look at how my worldview filters the rest of my life.

With my examples, I hope you get a better understanding of this whole worldview thing. Grab a piece of paper and a pen, and using these articles, try to determine your worldview using the seven to eight questions from Worldview Part 1 and Part 2. By the way, you don't have to agree with me.

Being a born-again Christian, my view of Reality, my ontology, is that there are natural and supernatural components to the universe around me. Even more than just believing, I know there are supernatural components. Can they be seen? Usually not. Can they be experienced? I have experienced them. They are not coincidences. If I get tied up in traffic and I'm late, there is a reason for that tardiness. There have been times when I was stopped dead in my tracks for something wholly inane, and then, driving by, saw a fender-bender or worse. On the positive side, I have listened to that still, small voice and made a different turn or decided to pop in on a friend, and it was a good choice; they desperately needed a sympathetic ear. Is this a "construct" of Romans 8:28? You decide.

I believe in a Personal God who sacrificed Himself to remove my sins and restore my fellowship with Him for all eternity. That gives me hope for my future and a strong belief that I must tell others out of love for them and God.

The nature of the Cosmos? I believe God created it all for His pleasure and glory. God has caused my eyes, and all my senses for that matter, to see and experience the beauty and complexity of the created universe. Too many times, I've been awestruck by a sunrise or sunset or a natural phenomenon. Looking at the rings around Saturn through a telescope while in college will stay in my mind forever.

Regarding humankind, I believe that men and women are created in the direct image of God. He created us male and female, and God didn't make a mistake when it came to my specific gender. Each of my three children, although all adopted, is a special gift from God to my wife and me. Are they always "good"? You've got to be kidding! They're human and sinful, but they carry God's image. And when I look into my grandson's eyes, I am humbled by this marvelous creation.

How do I look at people experiencing poverty? They may need a hand-up. How do I look at and work with a neurodiverse person when they come into my vehicle for a behind-the-wheel driving lesson? I'll do my absolute best to help them achieve that personal goal. These people have worth and value. They also are created in the image of God. How do I look at the rich man or woman? They put their pants on one leg at a time. They have to use the bathroom as I do. They, too, are created in the image of God. How do I look at the Muslim (or Hindu, Buddhist, Sikh, and others)? They are also sinners like me and need a Savior, the Lord Jesus. Every man, woman, and child walking the earth is created in the image of God.

The sick or elderly have unique places in my heart and life. Until God Himself takes them, they have a purpose to their last breath. I believe in the sanctity and sacredness of life. I weep for the lost man or woman participating in the gay lifestyle because they don't see, know, or understand the truly fulfilling and abundant life that God has prepared for them. Abortion? It's an abomination because that "blob of tissue" can only be a forming human being. Let it come to term for the purpose God had intended. What about a developing baby with potential defects? Let it come to term for the purpose God had intended. A family member's first child was born with severe defects: she had minimal digestive organs and only a brain stem. This newborn baby could not eat. We didn't think she would survive more than a day or two. She lived 10 days. Although I never saw her, my dad said she had a beautiful smile. My dad made it into his early seventies, battling cancer for several years. My mom, on the other hand, lived into her late nineties with dementia. As she spent her final months living with us, my children and I had the privilege of tending to her daily needs until she passed quietly into eternity one late autumn day. We are fearfully and wonderfully made (Psalm 139:14).

Upon my death, I know that I will pass into God's eternal presence based not on my "good" works (there are definitely some filthy rags there) but only because I trusted Jesus Christ as my Savior and Lord. His substitutionary death on the cross removed all of my sins - past, present, and future - and made me "right" before God. And I had to make that decision. I couldn't go on the coattails of past Christian family members; the choice was solely mine. Accept God and His free gift of Salvation or perish. I'll take Jesus any day.

What's my epistemology? What or how do I know what I know? God has given me plenty of opportunities to see Him at work. I have seen Him work in, around, and through me. By His hand, I have gained much, and I have also lost much: physically (my own health requiring several somewhat lengthy hospitalizations), personally (the death of my wife), and financially (business and property).

When I trusted God and His knowledge and wisdom through all these trials, God has *never* let me down. I can still stand and proclaim His love, His provision, and His guidance. I do not unquestioningly trust Him or His Word. Like the sage of antiquity, Job, I may have questioned certain events, but God has lovingly answered and shown me my proper place in His Plan. Throughout the Scriptures, God has asked us to test Him for ourselves. When we do, we find He is not only True but also Truth itself. I also know what I know through reasoning, logic, and observation of the world and universe around me.

My morality and ethics? There are times when I would say, "Don't ask." But seriously, I believe in absolutes. There exists right and wrong. Good and evil. Morality and ethics must come from Someone. Although raised in a relatively sheltered life, I knew that men or women were left to their own devices and would only stray to the bad. Heck, I am more prone to stray to my natural evil desires. It takes work to be "good." I choose God's standards because they are fair, just, and moral. I encourage my children or colleagues at work to follow through with specific undeserved kindnesses to someone who may have hurt us personally or corporately just because it's the right thing to do. Scripture tells us that it rains on the "just and the unjust," as God is Just to all (Matthew 5:45). But when I stumble and fall into sin (evil), I know that I can repent and return to God who loves me.

Going further down this road, I don't buy into the idea of "what's right for you may not be right for me." Well, why not? Simply because it doesn't make sense. If there is no standard, there is chaos. God intentionally built into us the conscience of knowing the difference between right and wrong. The statement above is for the person who would rather suppress Truth because it doesn't fit into what they want to do or how they want to act. Keep in mind that God's standards are impossible to keep. But that's okay. He keeps knocking on our hearts' doors, wanting a personal relationship.

What is my sense of History? At a little past middle age (I doubt I'll live to be 100...), I see that history is His story. God's fingerprints are all over my life, as I have already stated or alluded to. When I walked close to Him, God blessed me. When I have strayed, He has sometimes brought discipline and consequences. When I've struggled, I look back and see that He has carried me through. In hindsight, a decade of struggles and loss has been divine pruning to conform me more to the image of Christ. I am not the same man I was fifteen years ago, and I am eternally grateful. Perhaps you, too, are in the midst of a time of struggle and transformation, whether financial, relational, social, or even spiritual. Remember that hindsight is always 20/20.

Furthermore, I have witnessed purpose in my life. Because God has given me a glimpse of Himself, I know beyond a shadow of doubt that I am living in early 21st century America, was married to a wonderful woman, have three gifted children (each in their own ways), and am being used in my current employment for something that I would have never guessed or imagined doing. God has shown me wonders that are also gifts. He even gave me the time and will to do all this writing. Writing to encourage or teach you, the reader. Writing to be left as a legacy to someone in some other time or place.

What is my commitment? I'm all in for Jesus. At a very salient point in Jesus's ministry, it appeared that everything would go off the rails. Followers were walking away; some were disheartened, and others were disillusioned because they thought Jesus was in their midst for an entirely different reason. Still others were "afraid" of being with this rabbi whom the "powers that be" were out to not only bring down but to kill. When these people left, there were thirteen people left standing. Jesus offered (offers) eternal life, not guaranteeing a simple or easy life following Him.

Here's what happened, reading John 6:53-69:

"So Jesus said to them, 'Truly, truly, I say to you, unless you eat the flesh of the Son of Man and drink his blood, you have no life in you. Whoever feeds on my flesh and drinks my blood

has eternal life, and I will raise him up on the last day. For my flesh is true food, and my blood is true drink. Whoever feeds on my flesh and drinks my blood abides in me, and I in him. As the living Father sent me, and I live because of the Father, so whoever feeds on me, he also will live because of me. This is the bread that came down from heaven, not like the bread the fathers ate, and died. Whoever feeds on this bread will live forever.' Jesus said these things in the synagogue, as he taught at Capernaum.

"When many of his disciples heard it, they said, 'This is a hard saying; who can listen to it?' But Jesus, knowing in himself that his disciples were grumbling about this, said to them, 'Do you take offense at this? Then what if you were to see the Son of Man ascending to where he was before? It is the Spirit who gives life; the flesh is no help at all. The words that I have spoken to you are spirit and life. But there are some of you who do not believe.' (For Jesus knew from the beginning who those were who did not believe, and who it was who would betray him.) And he said, 'This is why I told you that no one can come to me unless it is granted him by the Father.

"After this, many of his disciples turned back and no longer walked with him. So Jesus said to the twelve, 'Do you want to go away as well?' Simon Peter answered him, 'Lord, to whom shall we go? You have the words of eternal life, and we have believed, and have come to know, that you are the Holy One of God.'"

It always boils down to this: What do you do with Jesus? It's all or nothing. There's no partial walk with Him.

So, what is my worldview? I have been called a "Pollyanna" many times. If so, so be it. The bottom line of my worldview is that God has given me life to live and a purpose for Him. I don't know everything, nor do I want to. In the end, I know one thing: God is good all of the time.

Lesson 11 - The Unbeliever's Worldview

The Christian worldview of life is straightforward for all intents and purposes. It's not that believers are automatons, but we "view" the world and universe around us through the only eyes that matter: God's eyes.

On the other hand, the unbeliever looks at the world very differently. He looks at it through his own eyes. Virtually everything he (or she) sees or experiences - visible and invisible, perceived and actual, logical and illogical - is seen through their personal filter.

There is no single "unbeliever's" worldview. Like Paul in first-century Athens dealing with Epicureans and Stoics (Acts 17), the Apostle understood the basic tenets of their philosophy of living and could reason and persuasively argue with these "learned" men.

So, what are Epicureans and Stoics, you ask? Epicurus formulated the Epicurean philosophy around 307 BCE. Epicureans attacked supernatural and divine intervention. They sought "modest living" (everything in moderation) to attain a state of "tranquility" and freedom from fear, although this moderation bordered on the verge of asceticism. They typically followed an austere lifestyle.

Stoicism - founded by Zeno of Citium about 200 BCE - dealt with and concerned itself more with how a person behaved and sought to eliminate destructive emotions. Ultimately, the person practicing Stoicism would reach the level of "sage" (a person of moral and intellectual perfection) and, therefore, not suffer such emotions. For you Star Trek fans, think of the Vulcans.

The foundations of these ancient philosophies are still around today and provide the building blocks for the modern worldviews we see in society. There are many unbelieving worldviews, but thankfully, they fall into a few basic categories. Like Paul, we 21st-century believers must know who our audience is and grasp what they believe so that we may properly engage them in the reasoning of the Gospel.

When you ask the question: "what is the Nature of...?" as we did in looking at the Christian worldview, you'll find that the three most important questions that make the unbeliever "who" they are, are the questions of Ontology or reality, Epistemology or "knowing what you know" and Commitment. Let's go through these questions again from a Western (we will not concern ourselves with Eastern beliefs in this study, but for further information, I would encourage you to read James Sire's book, "The Universe Next Door"), unbelieving or non-Christian standpoint. Let's keep Romans 1:18 - 25 in mind, as it refers back to the chapter on the Unbelieving Mind.

First, what is the person's Ontology, or how do they view reality and God? How does that "spiritual" person describe or define God (if not in a Biblical Christian understanding and context).

What or how does that person of view understand Jesus Christ (God incarnate) and by the indwelling of the Holy Spirit in the born-again believer's life? We will look at the question of the belief in the afterlife when we come to the question of History.

The unbeliever is more of a naturalist or materialist - you can discuss Cosmology here, too. What matters to them is what they can see, touch, or experience. Whether with their own eyes or senses, through a microscope or telescope, they only see what "is." The "supernatural" doesn't, and you could probably go so far as to say "can't" exist. If there's no knowledge or desire to accept the possibility of the supernatural, then miracles are impossible, and God and the spirit realm don't exist. If they don't exist, it's easy to throw out a literal - and Biblical - six-day Creation, young earth theory, Biblical stories of the parting of the Red Sea, the sun standing still, the Virgin Birth, and the Resurrection. Those are just stories made up by "unlearned" people of past millennia to explain natural phenomena or support their beliefs. That is their "meta-narrative".

From naturalists comes the idea of "nihilism": we've come from nothing, and that's where we're all headed. Nothing matters. There's no purpose (question 6: Teleology). There's no meaning to life. Everything that we see and experience is a product of "chance."

What is the person's view of Cosmology or the universe around us? Where did all of what we see, experience, and can't come from? If their belief is ex nihilo (out of nothing), what caused everything? And not only the natural world but the laws that govern this natural world. The laws of physics, mathematics, chemistry, and other sciences govern the orderliness of the universe around us. Where did those universal laws come from? Can orderliness come from chaos or disorderliness? If there are laws, there must be a lawgiver.

In his denial of God and anything supernatural, the idea of "Science" comes into play. Science can become the "god" of the unbeliever. Although science has been around and used for thousands of years, the ideas of the process of evolution and the "Big Bang" theory are not even centuries old. Until the mid to late 1800s, the general belief was that God (sometimes god) created all and put it into motion. Being sophisticated, modern men and women, well, that just couldn't be. New "constructs" (stories - backed up by "science") were needed. I remember being in elementary school in the late 1960s and early 1970s, being taught in our science class that the universe was about three to five billion years old. Today, the number is up to ten times that. Why? Did science need more time for its evolutionary processes to take place?

When you watch television shows about the creation of the universe on Discovery or History International, you see "educated" men and women spouting "facts" about what happened so many eons ago. Were they there? Was anyone there to corroborate those facts? Of course not. So then, how can they be so sure of their beliefs? These scientists must have great faith.

The third and fourth questions we ask are, "What is the nature of anthropology or man?" How does the person view life and death? Are we simply a mass of cells and crazy chemistry? In the Biblical view of man, God consults Himself (the three members of the Trinity) and then creates mankind in His (God's) image. Once again, we read in Genesis 1:26-28a, *"Then God said, 'Let us make man in Our image, after Our likeness. And let them have dominion over the fish of the sea and over the birds of the heavens and over the livestock and over all the earth and over every creeping thing that creeps on the earth.*

"So God created man in his own image, in the image of God he created him; male and female he created them.

"And God blessed them. And God said to them, "Be fruitful and multiply and fill the earth and subdue it,"

It is far easier to understand and believe (as it has for most of recorded history) that mankind was specially created. Evolution requires extreme "faith" to believe that for billions or at least hundreds of millions of years, atoms (wherever those came from) formed molecules, eventually becoming proteins and cells, resulting in life. And this is just the biological aspect.

Where do logical thought processes, poetry, artistry, imagination, storytelling, music, the understanding and manipulation of the sciences, farming, and even religion come from through evolution? How about understanding love, beauty, justice, mercy, creativity, and forgiveness; how does evolution bring about any of these?

As Biblical Christians, we are thankful that God chose to communicate or share these attributes with His creation, specifically because we are created in His image and likeness.

Many non-Christians believe that the Bible and Biblical Christians "subjugate" women when, in reality, God specifically formed women to be helpmates and, therefore, "complete" men. A mature Christian man will readily admit that his female wife blesses his life. Quoting novelist William Golding: *"If you give her sperm, she will give you a baby. If you give her a house, she will give you a home. If you give her groceries, she will give you a meal. If you give her a smile, she will give you her heart."*

In Christianity, whether you choose to believe it correctly or not, God has created the sexes "equally"; in other words, men and women are created in the image of God. We are two separate, distinct sexes made to complement one another. Women make terrific teachers and praise leaders within the church body. Women have provided wonderful counsel to many men.

Throughout the New Testament, women are treated with high regard and respect (especially by Jesus Himself); just do a quick read through the Gospels and the Book of Acts. Women may be "commanded" to submit to their husbands, but our job as husbands is a huge responsibility to protect our wives and keep them holy, even to death (Ephesians 5:22 - 33). That's a high calling.

Looking at the other questions of Nature, what does the unbeliever do with those questions of Morality and Ethics? For the naturalist or realist, it becomes a question of relativity: what's true (real or good) for me may or may not be true (real or good) for you.

Whatever works, you know? So, where did morality and ethics come from? What of the ideas of good and evil, right or wrong? Sacred and profane? Why is it "wrong" or "evil" if someone steals a poor old woman's purse and then "right" or "good" when another individual gets it back? Who sets the rules or the standards of morality and ethics? Is it society in general or the individual? Do they change, or are the standards of right and wrong, good and evil "immutable" (as is God)? More importantly, how do you live under those conditions?

Here, we deal with the philosophy of Existentialism. According to Answers.com, Existentialism is a *"philosophy that emphasizes the uniqueness and isolation of the individual experience in a hostile or indifferent universe, regards human existence as unexplainable, and stresses freedom of choice and responsibility for the consequences of one's acts."* Again, "chance" is the "power" behind all that is. Do what you want; you're not necessarily responsible for it.

Imagine playing a game of chess. There are rules. Certain pieces can move in specific ways, directions, and spaces. You are playing by the rules, but your opponent keeps changing them to suit their fancy. Suddenly, a pawn can move like a Queen or a knight like a rook. Never mind the game's fairness, but what can you count on with the passing of each move? If you're going to live by "chance," then you have to be willing to be on this unending roller coaster of uncertainty for your entire existence. You can't pick and choose when the rules apply and when they don't.

Back in the early 1980s, at the urging of a close acquaintance, I participated in the "est" Training (later known as the Forum and then Landmark Forum). Looking back, it was a remarkable two weekends of my time well spent. I saw and experienced many things in very different lights. My mind may have broadened, and my thinking expanded, but the anchor of standards was severed. I was set "free" from the bondage of "old thinking." I could create my own reality. It would be cool if the 'Training' could be done in a 'Christian' context. People could break away from their old notions and find liberty and 'new truth'." I now realize that the "Training" took you off of one hamster wheel of living and put you onto another. The real problem was that the new wheel had no tether to Truth.

So next up - and tied into this idea of morality - is a person's Epistemology (question 5). How does an unbeliever, naturalist, or relativist "know what they know?" Where did they get their information? Not to be snarky, but they obviously weren't there at the "Big Bang." They didn't see the ooze become a microorganism, then a fish, and so on up the evolutionary scale until it reached man. But this is again where "Science" comes in. Although the unbeliever will not admit it, much "faith" is also needed. They have to have faith and a strong commitment to their beliefs and sources of information. Moreover, what are the authorities or credentials of the naturalist? How have those sources changed over time? If the "authority" is the diorama in the museum or the program on PBS, what's their authority?

For the Biblical Christian, all of the answers that a human being needs to live life as completely as possible in this temporal realm can be found in the pages between Genesis 1:1 and Revelation 22:21. Most answers are direct, and many answers are alluded to (for example, smoking or tattoos). How we treat our bodies (temples of the Holy Spirit), how we interact with the world around us, the plant and animal kingdoms, and the general environment (stewardship because God put mankind in charge of all of these areas) are all answered in the pages of Scripture. And the list goes on.

What is "Truth"? That discussion has been on the agenda for millennia. As noted before, even Pontius Pilate asked Jesus, "What is truth?" Jesus gave him an answer, but he chose to sidestep the issue. We'll look at this idea at another time.

Through all of this, we haven't even begun to look at the ideas of hope, love, or emotions. Why are humans the only creatures on Earth that have emotions? Now, I know that your pet may whine when you leave it and be "happy" when you return (my dogs certainly do!), but why do they do that? Do pets have the capacity to understand good and evil?

What is your Purpose in life (Teleology)? As a Biblical Christian, I have purpose. I am an "integral" part of God's Plan. That may sound or appear egotistical, but I understand that there's something more significant than my life in 21st century America.

How many people "live" aimlessly, wandering from job to job or relationship to relationship, trying to figure themselves out, living and looking but never "finding" themselves?

Through the chapters of this book, I have stated or alluded to the various turns my life has taken. As this study is being finalized, I find myself doing tasks and affecting other people in ways I could have never dreamed of five or ten years ago, never mind half a life ago. God has brought me through many trials, struggles, successes, and victories over the decades that are finally being put to a greater purpose, a greater use, for His Kingdom and glory.

Can an unbeliever state that they've made a difference for eternity? Has God somehow provided you with a purpose that He will use for His plans that will affect others for eternity?

The Biblical Christian can rely on the Bible regarding the nature of history. Modern archaeology, geology, and other sciences have affirmed and confirmed the reliability of the Biblical account of creation and the history of man from creation to today.

From the prophecies of the rise of nations and empires mentioned in the book of Daniel to the hundreds of prophecies pointing to the coming of Jesus, which have been fulfilled in incredible detail and exactitude, the Bible, the Word of God, has been completed. Outside sources have confirmed historical figures such as King David and Pontius Pilate. The veracity of the Scriptures continues to be well documented. And based on that past history, we can rely on it to look into the future.

So, how does the unbeliever view history? Where do they get their "facts"? Can those facts be verified, or is it speculation and conjecture? How many outside sources corroborate those facts?

Finally, we come to the matter of Commitment. How committed is the unbeliever to their worldview?

Throughout history, we can recount how various people recanted their stories or testimonies because they either lacked commitment or those testimonies wouldn't or couldn't stand up to cross-examination and scrutiny.

Today, as in Jesus' day, many were accused of pushing or accepting "conspiracy" theories. Oftentimes, those theories prove themselves trustworthy. The committed believer whose life has been changed by and through an acknowledgment of the Gospel of Jesus Christ forms the solid foundation of our commitment. We can verify what God has done supernaturally in many of our lives.

American attorney and special counsel to former President Richard Nixon, Charles (Chuck) Colson was part of the cover-up of the Watergate scandal. After serving time in prison (guilty of "obstruction of justice") for his crimes, Colson later founded the ministry of Prison Fellowship. During his time in prison, Chuck repented of his sins and committed his life to Jesus Christ. God used this broken man to lead many to Christ over the years. Colson wrote about the Bible, especially Jesus and His finished work at the Cross: "*I know the resurrection is a fact, and Watergate proved it to me. How? Because 12 men testified they had seen Jesus raised from the dead, then they proclaimed that truth for 40 years, never once denying it. Every one was beaten, tortured, stoned and put in prison. They would not have endured that if it weren't true. Watergate embroiled 12 of the most powerful men in the world-and they couldn't keep a lie for three weeks. You're telling me 12 apostles could keep a lie for 40 years? Absolutely impossible.*"

Finally, when it comes to the commitment of the unbeliever, especially those isms we've been looking at, they are left with how to live out these worldviews. How committed are they to these worldview constructs? Can they truly live with some of these views? I propose that it would be difficult at best. I know that I can live day to day with my worldviews. The various parts of my worldview do not compete with or contradict one another. My belief in a personal God supports all aspects of my worldview.

Lesson 11 – From Doubt to Defense – The Unbeliever's Worldview

Verses: Romans 1:18 – 23, Acts 17:13 – 34

Key Questions:

How do Christian and non-Christian worldviews differ?
Can a person's worldview change or be changed?

Facts are interpreted by our worldview.

What were the beliefs of the Epicureans and Stoics of first-century Athens?

Epicureans –

Stoics -

A person's Worldview is made up of how we view the world around us. We look at the world around us by answering the questions: "What is the Nature of…"

1. Ontology

2. Cosmology

3. Anthropology

4. Epistemology

5. Ethics

6. Teleology (purpose)

8. Commitment

If "chance" and "chaos" is the basis of the unbeliever's worldview, are they able to live out these worldview ideas?

The Gospel vs. the Hamster Wheel of the "isms"

Other "isms" and "theisms."

Living in early 21st-century Western society, we are surrounded by and sometimes pressured by worldviews that oppose a Biblically orthodox worldview.

So what are these other "isms"?

Before continuing, to be fair, whatever worldview you hold, you ultimately desire to influence or change people and, therefore, the world around you. This idea is also so for unbelievers (atheists and agnostics), Christians, Jews, Far Eastern adherents of Hinduism, Buddhism, etc., as well as post-modernists and any other philosophy that you want to discuss.

Even in the realm of Christianity, there are "isms" that range from, let's say, "squishy" to downright heretical. In their zeal to be more "inclusive" or "relevant" to the world around them or the communities they serve, many denominations have effectively diluted or undermined the message of God's Word in general and Jesus's Gospel in particular.

This discussion will use a very broad brush, and the intent is not to cast false aspersions or slander any of these belief systems but to cause you, the reader, to see that there are significant differences in their worldview. The discussion will also be very cursory; there isn't enough space or time or my understanding to provide a complete picture of many of the "isms." When defending the Christian Faith, we must know how and what our neighbors think and believe. We need to understand what they think and how they think about it.

In each of these "isms" or worldviews, especially those that point to the promise of an actual afterlife, there is or appears to be a new "hamster wheel" of works in which a person must participate to merit somehow an afterlife of "paradise" or "heaven" or "nirvana."

Each worldview competes for your attention and your belief in it. If you accept a person's or society's worldview, that's fine. However, if you don't, that's your business; go in peace. Some of these "isms" may be "tolerant" of Christianity and allow an attitude of mutual "agree to disagree" relationship. Certain "isms" are directly hostile to Christianity, including some that we may have considered as a distant family relation. "Isms" such as communism, atheism, egalitarianism, Islamism, and even within Talmudic or Rabbinic Judaism, at the least, would like to see Christianity pushed aside, if not obliterated.

Over the centuries, we've seen that when Christians go out of their comfort zone into "unreached" parts of the globe to fulfill the Great Commission (Matthew 28:), sometimes those missionaries are met with outright hostility, where the missionaries are summarily slaughtered (for example, animist tribes in the jungles of the Amazon or Borneo). Sometimes, those missionaries were welcomed with the idea of trade and commerce (for instance, in imperial Japan and China of the 15th and 16th centuries CE).

Let me state here and now that, at my core, I do not like confrontation, whether personal or business. I want to get along with everyone I encounter, regardless of the situation or circumstance.

Recently, a couple of dear friends challenged me with my use of certain terms and beliefs. These friends and brothers in Christ have caused me to think more critically about the Bible and God's calling on His creation and even consider some of the terminology I use. For example, I'm more inclined to say "Biblical-Christian" rather than a Judeo-Christian tradition. Biblical Christianity relies on the entire text of the Old and New Testaments, from Genesis to Revelation, which is God's whole Word to us. We have to rely on the entirety of the Scriptures, in their context, not only on the parts that we "accept" or "like."

All of the Old Testament Patriarchs and Prophets (Adam, Noah, Abraham, Isaac, Jacob, David, Isaiah, Jeremiah, Daniel, etc.) could be considered "pre-Christians" in that "by faith" they wholly followed (obeyed and submitted) God, His Law, His instructions to them (although with flaws) to the best of their abilities. The writer of the Book of Hebrews, chapter eleven, includes these names and others who "by faith" realized and understood (at least partially) their part in God's Plan for His Creation, including our fall, repentance, redemption, and restoration through Jesus the Messiah. We read in Hebrews 11:1-7, 32-40, 12:1-3: *"Now faith is the assurance of things hoped for, the conviction of things not seen. For by it the people of old received their commendation. By faith we understand that the universe was created by the word of God, so that what is seen was not made out of things that are visible.*

"By faith Abel offered to God a more acceptable sacrifice than Cain, through which he was commended as righteous, God commending him by accepting his gifts. And through his faith, though he died, he still speaks. By faith Enoch was taken up so that he should not see death, and he was not found, because God had taken him. Now before he was taken he was commended as having pleased God. And without faith it is impossible to please him, for whoever would draw near to God must believe that he exists and that he rewards those who seek him. By faith Noah, being warned by God concerning events as yet unseen, in reverent fear constructed an ark for the saving of his household. By this he condemned the world and became an heir of the righteousness that comes by faith...

"And what more shall I say? For time would fail me to tell of Gideon, Barak, Samson, Jephthah, of David and Samuel and the prophets— who through faith conquered kingdoms, enforced justice, obtained promises, stopped the mouths of lions, quenched the power of fire, escaped the edge of the sword, were made strong out of weakness, became mighty in war, put foreign armies to flight. Women received back their dead by resurrection. Some were tortured, refusing to accept release, so that they might rise again to a better life. Others suffered mocking and flogging, and even chains and imprisonment. They were stoned, they were sawn in two, they were killed with the sword. They went about in skins of sheep and goats, destitute, afflicted, mistreated—of whom the world was not worthy—wandering about in deserts and mountains, and in dens and caves of the earth.

"And all these, though commended through their faith, did not receive what was promised, since God had provided something better for us, that apart from us they should not be made perfect.

"Therefore, since we are surrounded by so great a cloud of witnesses, let us also lay aside every weight, and sin which clings so closely, and let us run with endurance the race that is set before us, looking to Jesus, the founder and perfecter of our faith, who for the joy that was set before him endured the cross, despising the shame, and is seated at the right hand of the throne of God.

"Consider him who endured from sinners such hostility against himself, so that you may not grow weary or fainthearted."

These pre-Christian saints believed in and trusted all that God had done, was doing, and would do by faith alone, and God credited that faith to them as righteousness. In every sense of the idea, these men and women were Christians, holding a Biblical and Christian worldview. As history and the Bible point out, when Messiah (Jesus) finally arrived to the Hebrew people (as prophesied), He was summarily rejected. The expectation that Messiah would save them from "Roman oppression" was misunderstood as Jesus had come to save the lost (both Jew and Gentile), not from temporal oppression, but from the sin that separates everyone from God Himself.

Although some saw and recognized Who Jesus was and understood His work, the vast majority rejected Him and rejected Him to the point of the people in chorus shouting out to Pontius Pilate (who recognized His innocence) at His trial, *"...all the people answered, 'His blood be on us and on our children!'" Then he released for them Barabbas, and having scourged Jesus, delivered him to be crucified."* Matthew 27:25-26.

Jesus was in their midst, regularly performing signs, miracles, and wonders, and most rejected Him. We note that the "devout" and learned Jews of that day, who cross-referenced their Scriptures in real time, chose to deny Jesus's gift of eternal life by Faith and instead clung to "tradition" and the Law. The people chose their version of the hamster wheel of performing works.

Jesus summarized the entire Law and the Prophets into two commandments: Love God by willingly obeying, repenting of personal and corporate sin, and submitting to God; love others by willingly serving, caring for, and honoring (the dignity of the human person created in the image and likeness of God); and make disciples by sharing the good news of Jesus's finished work.

So, what does all of this have to do with a hamster wheel? True and Biblical Christianity, contrary to what many believe, is not a punch list of "do's and don'ts." Believers love others as an outflowing of our love for God. A believer's "works" are not "works" as much as they are "fruit." Our faith is made manifest in our "works". James, the half-brother of Jesus (it took him a while to understand Jesus as well), puts faith and works into their proper context:

"What good is it, my brothers, if someone says he has faith but does not have works? Can that faith save him? If a brother or sister is poorly clothed and lacking in daily food, and one of you says to them, 'Go in peace, be warmed and filled,' without giving them the things needed for the body, what good is that? So also faith by itself, if it does not have works, is dead.

"But someone will say, 'You have faith and I have works.' Show me your faith apart from your works, and I will show you my faith by my works. You believe that God is one; you do well. Even the demons believe—and shudder!" James 2:14-19

The Biblical Christian (properly discipled) has discovered that they are living a lifestyle of relationship to God, rather than a hamster wheel of works "hoping" somehow that they'll be rewarded. As has already been stated, as Biblical Christians, we understand the following simple terms of our faith as demonstrated through the example of the Roman's Road to Salvation:

1. Every human being who has ever lived, is living, and will ever live is a sinner, and our lives fall short of God's perfection and expectation of perfection (God's perfect holiness). No one is righteous. None of us parents have had to teach our children how to disobey, as this unrighteousness is a part of us. "None is righteous, no, not one; no one understands; no one seeks for God." Romans 3:10. "…for all have sinned and fall short of the glory of God," Romans 3:23.

2. Since God's standard is perfection, not one of us can meet that standard and, therefore, due His punishment, which is eternal death, both physical and spiritual. *"For the wages of sin is death…"* Romans 6:23a

3. As we are all created in God's image and likeness (only humans bear this image and likeness), He still cares for us and desires a complete and eternal relationship. Therefore, God is willing to provide a way to restore that relationship. In His love for His image-bearing creation, God Himself provides the way of restoration. *"For while we were still weak, at the right time Christ died for the ungodly. For one will scarcely die for a righteous person—though perhaps for a good person one would dare even to die—but God shows his love for us in that while we were still sinners, Christ died for us."* Romans 5:6-8, *"…but the free gift of God is eternal life in Christ Jesus our Lord."* Romans 6:23b

4. God knew and knows that it is impossible to work our way to Salvation and, therefore, eternal life. All one has to do is read and think through all the various laws and sacrifices outlined in the books of Exodus, Leviticus, and Deuteronomy. It is impossible to satisfy God's demands of atonement fully, so He offers a way through simple belief and reception of Himself (like those pre-Christian saints). Like the thief on the cross next to Jesus at Calvary, he knew he was a sinner and recognized Jesus as the only way to Salvation and eternal life. *"...if you confess with your mouth that Jesus is Lord and believe in your heart that God raised him from the dead, you will be saved. For with the heart one believes and is justified, and with the mouth one confesses and is saved. For the Scripture says, 'Everyone who believes in him will not be put to shame.' For there is no distinction between Jew and Greek; for the same Lord is Lord of all, bestowing his riches on all who call on him. For 'everyone who calls on the name of the Lord will be saved.'"* Romans 10:9-13; Jesus is the only way to eternal life as He said, *"I am the way, and the truth, and the life. No one comes to the Father except through Me."* John 14:6

5. We can only experience true forgiveness of sin and restoration of relationship with the hope of eternal life through the atoning finished work of Jesus on the Cross. Even Jesus's final words before He breathed His last were these: *"it is finished."* The debt for all who would believe is now paid in full through His bloody sacrifice, with nothing else for us to do except believe and accept His free gift. *"Therefore, since we have been justified by faith, we have peace with God through our Lord Jesus Christ."* Romans 5:1. Romans 8:1-4 goes on to affirm this with Paul writing, *"There is therefore now no condemnation for those who are in Christ Jesus. For the law of the Spirit of life has set you free in Christ Jesus from the law of sin and death. For God has done what the law, weakened by the flesh, could not do. By sending his own Son in the likeness of sinful flesh and for sin, he condemned sin in the flesh, in order that the righteous requirement of the law might be fulfilled in us, who walk not according to the flesh but according to the Spirit."*

And nothing will or can stand in the way of that restored relationship. Paul underlines how supernatural Jesus salvation is when he states, *"For I am sure that neither death nor life, nor angels nor rulers, nor things present nor things to come, nor powers, nor height nor depth, nor anything else in all creation, will be able to separate us from the love of God in Christ Jesus our Lord."* Romans 8:38-39

And now, we are to abide and trust in His Sovereignty alone. We Christians have no "hamster wheel." Through the power of the Holy Spirit, who lives within every believer, we can regularly say "no" to sin and its consequences and "yes" to loving God and our fellow human beings.

The bottom-line question we are to ask, which is to be answered, is this: What will you do about Jesus? The answer is either yes or no; there is no middle ground. Either He is your Savior and Redeemer, or He is not. Regardless of your answer, Jesus is still and always has been LORD.

Every other "ism" has the individual, and even the collective, working toward "salvation" or "nirvana" or whatever they choose to call it. The doing, whether it is good works (you name the work), fulfilling sacrifices at a temple, or fulfilling and keeping sacraments (i.e., infant baptism, Eucharist, orders, etc.), is not what admits you into God's eternal Kingdom. Perhaps it's doing nothing because they believe that, in the end, there is nothing to do or to be.

Back to a couple of other "isms." Existentialism has led to postmodernism. Postmodernism looks at all we have discussed and then goes a step further, stating, "I'll create my own reality." When you create your own reality, what is the purpose? Is there a purpose? The postmodernist has to ask the question (as did a former President of the United States), "What is the meaning of 'is'?"

The post-modern thinker (committed person, question 7 or 8) constructs a history or personal story that matches up with their belief system. It's their "meta-narrative." It may not have one piece of truth or historicity, but it's "true for them."

The entire LGBTQ plus agenda discussion is a current example of "creating your own reality."

So, what is an unbeliever's or an atheist's worldview? Why is there an animosity toward theism, God, and Christian theism? Aldous Huxley, an existentialist of the 20th century, is quoted as saying, *"For myself, no doubt for most of my contemporaries, the philosophy of meaninglessness was essentially an instrument of liberation. The liberation we desired was ... from a certain system of morality. We objected to the morality because it interfered with our sexual freedom."* Quoted by Stanley L. Jaki, Cosmos and Creator (Edinburgh: Scottish Academic Press, 1980).

This philosophy is the overarching mindset that then demands abortion, homosexual "rights," and promotes other deviant behaviors. Pedophilia (sexual attraction to prepubescent children) and hebephilia (sexual attraction to adolescents) are two examples. Then there is the discussion of extreme "abortion" of children up to the age of three (used at one time in Germany) because "they're not really human," population control (the idea that the earth is "over"-populated), and even eugenics (selective breeding of humans).

Rev. E. Paul Hovey (1908-1996) succinctly puts it this way: *"Men do not reject the Bible because it contradicts itself, but because it contradicts them."*

In other words, they don't want to live and function within transcendent objective laws and rules or be reminded of sin. They want to be able to do what they want, with whom they want, and when they want, without worrying about consequences; the key phrase is "worry." If there are no absolutes, God, purpose, or meaning, do what you want to whomever you want. Since there are no absolutes, there are few consequences - according to your beliefs.

But maybe existentialist extraordinaire - and committed atheist - Jean-Paul Sartre put it best. Yet again, keep in mind Romans 1:18-25 as you read his thoughts from his autobiography. *"I had been playing with matches and burned a small rug. I was in the process of covering up my crime when suddenly God saw me. I felt His gaze inside my head and on my hands... I flew into a rage against so crude an indiscretion, I blasphemed... He never looked at me again... I had the more difficulty getting rid of Him* [the Holy Ghost] *in that He had installed Himself at the back of my head... I collared the Holy Ghost in the cellar and threw Him out."* Sartre later writes: *"Atheism is a cruel affair. I still write. What else can I do?"* The Words (New York: George Braziller, 1964).

The real bottom-line question is this, and the answer is binary:

What are you going to do with Jesus? Accept Him or Reject Him.

Lesson 12 - Actions and Attitudes

The Book of Acts shows our early Christian brethren, primarily Peter and Paul, reasoning, debating, and even arguing with unbelievers.

Their purpose? It wasn't to argue people into the Kingdom of God, show themselves as superior in knowledge or faith, or boast. The ultimate purpose of the discussions and arguments was to present God in the way God presents Himself in the Bible.

Do we reason, debate, and argue with the unbelieving world? Yes. Are people argued or debated into a saving knowledge of Jesus Christ and, therefore, into the Kingdom of God? No. No one is argued or debated into God's Eternal Kingdom.

The Blood of Christ saves people who come into the Kingdom only as the Spirit of God prompts, leads, and directs. God stimulates the individual's spirit, creates the person's interests, reveals Himself to the person, and saves them. You and I are privileged instruments in His plan.

God expects us to understand our audience and be *"...prepared to make a defense to anyone who asks you for a reason for the hope that is in you; yet do it with gentleness and respect,"* 1 Peter 3:15. How do we do this?

Before we get to those discussions, we still need to understand more of our audience. What is our Epistemology? How do we "know what we know?" What forms the basis for our "facts?" Let's look at two "foundations" for thought: the Myths of Neutrality and Autonomy.

Neutrality is self-explanatory. We want to be "neutral" in our understanding and approach. The problem is the idea of neutrality itself: how are we to be neutral in our Christianity? We shouldn't be! And how can non-Christians be neutral in their atheism or agnosticism? Our thinking and our worldview itself is one or the other. We must believe in God and His plan and purpose, or not. None of us are "neutral" in our beliefs and worldviews. There is no middle ground.

The atheist or agnostic (polite atheist) does not come to their belief system with an attitude of neutrality. They have a belief, a "faith." They are not neutral.

Even when presenting a logical argument for the Christian Faith, we cannot compromise. There is no middle ground. Think about it: how - or why - would you want to find a middle ground when defending God and His Word? We may compromise on many secular issues, but when dealing with matters of eternity and other people's very lives and souls, there is no compromise. Remember, Jesus Himself said, *"Whoever is not with me is against me, and whoever does not gather with me scatters."* Matthew 12:30. We are either eternally saved or eternally damned.

In another aspect of Neutrality, some want the "facts." "Just give me the facts," they say. They wish to be "objective" in their thinking and reasoning. While striving to be neutral, we massage the "facts" to fit our understanding, conclusions, and, therefore *our* reality. But remember, "Facts are stupid things..." Facts may be "neutral," but they have meaning when interpreted through our worldview. When we understand that idea, the entire quote reads, *"Facts are stupid things, until brought into connection with some general law,"* (naturalist Professor Louis Agassiz of Harvard in the 19th century). There must be a standard to measure or interpret the facts. As accurate as that idea is in biology, astronomy, and the rest of the sciences, it is with how we look at the world (reality) - and everything in it, what is seen and unseen - as revealed by God Himself. We choose to accept God's Revelation or not.

The unbeliever's true attitude is that they want "facts," but they want to be able to judge those facts according to what they believe is right or wrong. There is no neutrality.

Furthermore, although the Bible - God's Word - may not give us every possible "fact" of right or wrong, it provides us with the framework to think through an issue. If we know God and His Word, we "know" His mind. We understand what God means regarding sin or creation. And because God is Immutable or unchanging, what's true in one passage of Scripture is true elsewhere when understood in its context. Again, see Romans 1:18-23.

As we suppress God and His Revelation, we suppress Truth. We have to choose sides: good or evil, righteousness or unrighteousness, friend of God or enemy of God. Neutrality is a myth—neutrality crumbles.

And so, we are led to the myth of Autonomy. This so-called intellectual autonomy states that man is "autonomous" regarding "truth." It is man who is the arbiter of "truth." It is man who decides what is true or false. There is no standard of truth—or any standard for that matter. God is forsaken. Divine authority is dismissed. The fickleness of man reigns supreme.

What does this look like? An example would be someone who makes a claim that rejects the very existence of God. Okay. So then, what is their authority to make that claim? Since they have dismissed divine revelation (in general or special terms), how can they conclusively make the statement or claim that God doesn't exist? What is their proof? Are they going on their personal feelings or their perfect knowledge of the entirety of the known and unknown universe? What is their authority? How can they know?

By the same token, we, as believing Christians, may be asked the same question. Okay. In our case (mine, speaking personally), I have chosen to submit my puny authority (and autonomy) to the Divine Authority of Almighty God and His Word, the Bible. I am not autonomous in my thinking. I am not autonomous in my life. Instead, I rely entirely on God. Proverbs 1:7 says, "The fear of the LORD is the beginning of knowledge, but fools despise wisdom and instruction." It's a matter of the will. Because I have confidence in what God has done throughout history, as written in Scripture and backed up by non- or extra-Biblical historical and scientific evidence, as well as what He has done in my own life, I know that God is Truthful, Reliable, and Dependable.

Finally, what are our actions to be? In other words, how do we present our personal Apologetic? All of the arguments we've been discussing throughout this study may be intellectually intriguing, but so what? If I present this information or these arguments for the sake of being "right," then I have failed, and rightfully so.

Going back to 1 Peter 3:15, we are to give a reason for our hope. I have to confess that I've written various projects many times, thinking, "Boy, Ron, this is great stuff." In reality, I have to be reminded. Really? So, what of it? What is my motivation for presenting Christ? Am I doing it out of a boastful - and sinful - nature? If so, the words are hollow, and the voice is like a clanging cymbal. Am I spouting out Scripture with the attitude of looking for praise from other men and women rather than a desire that they (you), too, would come to a saving knowledge of Jesus Christ? If my sinful attitude is so, where's my love for you? As my friend Brad says, "Where's the grace?"

We share "hope" with others because we love others. We pray for opportunities to share the Goodness of God. We spend time in His Word to know God better and become more Christ-like in all aspects of our lives. We want to become more attractive to the people God has put into our lives in order to point them to God. Do we really want to be more like Jesus who, *"though he was in the form of God, did not count equality with God a thing to be grasped, but emptied himself, by taking the form of a servant, being born in the likeness of men. And being found in human form, he humbled himself by becoming obedient to the point of death, even death on a cross."* (Philippians 2:6-8)? Is that our (my) motivation?

At the beginning of this chapter, I said that it is God who saves. And so He does. God may use us, sometimes despite ourselves, but He uses us. And He wants us to be so polished that we can properly reflect who He is and then patiently, lovingly, prayerfully, and winsomely present His Gospel. Ultimately, God doesn't expect us to be perfect in appearance and presentation. He knows that I am not perfect. God simply wants us to be available (remember those first lessons on "showing up"), to speak truthfully of Him, and to be able to share His Gospel.

Let's Pray. Heavenly Father, thank you for using us to further your Kingdom; it is a mighty privilege. May our hearts and minds be used of You for Your Glory only. Amen.

Lesson 12 – From Doubt to Defense – Actions and Attitudes

Verses: 1 Peter 3:15, Acts 11:1-18; 17:1-9; 23:1-10; 24:24-27.

Key Questions:

Can we be neutral or autonomous in our thought?
How are we to present our Apologetic?

Myths.

Neutrality –

Autonomy -

Attitude check: My attitude determines my personal Apologetic.

How has your attitude changed through this study?

How has your attitude affected your walk with God?

What further changes would you like to see?

How does your attitude affect unbelievers?

Copyright© Ronald Parrs 2025

Lesson 13 - Apologetic Strategies

Although Apologetics may be a powerful argument, it is not the end of our discourse with the unbeliever.

Our apologetic must be the groundwork or foundation for Evangelism. In Chapters 25 and 26 of the Book of Acts, we see Paul before two powerful and influential leaders who, on the surface, hold Paul's life in their hands. However, as we Christians do, Paul knew that God held and controlled Paul's life. And Paul knew he had a mission: to spread the Gospel Truth of Jesus Christ to the world.

For about 30 years, God gave Paul the opportunity to preach His Gospel and, more importantly, get to know Him well. God personally taught Paul all that he needed to know with the instruction to "write it all down." His writings to the various churches he first led, answering their concerns or problems, were thoughtfully transcribed, inspired by the Holy Spirit, to codify Jesus's teaching. That command may not be in the Bible, but Paul knew what he had to do. He used his intellect. He used his knowledge of the Law and the Prophets (the Old Testament) to be the foundation of what he learned from the Lord Jesus as well as the eyewitness accounts of Peter, John, James, and others to "fill out" as it were, the information he needed to make his apologetic personal, accurate, thoughtful, cogent and articulate.

But more than anything else, God gave Paul a heart to follow Christ's command to reach the world with this special revelation. Before his death, Paul wrote the bulk of the New Testament. Today, we benefit not only from Paul's labors but also from his love for us.

But let's return to the discussion at hand.

In Acts Chapters 25 and 26, we see the apostle Paul under arrest by the Roman authorities. The Jewish leaders want Paul "extradited" to Jerusalem to face charges. As a good politician, Festus figures that there's something more and senses a certain deceitfulness of the Jewish leaders. In fact, Festus can't find any of the so-called charges to be true. Not having a Jewish worldview, Festus needs another set of eyes and ears to understand what is happening. Fortunately for him, the Jewish King Agrippa and his wife Bernice are visiting. Festus wants to understand what all the hubbub is about and convenes a hearing in their presence.

When Paul is brought in to defend himself, he is poised, calm, and, most of all, prepared. We can be sure that he was fervently praying for this time, for the right words and attitude, on all sides. Speaking directly to Agrippa, Paul goes through everything the King should know about Jewish history, teaching, and tradition. Paul directly engaged Agrippa. Knowing his audience, Paul presents the historical facts of Jesus' Life, Passion, and Resurrection and how those facts directly affected, influenced, and changed his life (Paul's personal apologetic).

Paul, better than any other person at the time, understood the noetic effects of sin. He understood that sin directly affects our mind and, therefore, our thinking regarding God and His revelation. Paul spoke effectively yet truthfully and forcefully. He didn't belittle or talk down to anyone. Paul also spoke lovingly. He wanted all who heard him that day (even the attending servants and guards) to, at some future point, come to a saving knowledge of God through Jesus Christ.

Paul, thanks to being brought up under the teaching of the great Jewish scholar and teacher (rabbi) Gamaliel, also understood the succinct strategy of Proverbs 26:4-5, which states, *"Answer not a fool according to his folly, lest you be like him yourself. Answer a fool according to his folly, lest he be wise in his own eyes."* At first glance, the two verses seem almost contradictory, but they're not. They are a tremendous strategy for presenting a good apologetic.

Let's look at those verses, and I know you will understand. *"Answer not a fool according to his folly, lest you be like him yourself."* In other words, when a "fool" (unbeliever) is speaking with you foolishly, you are not to join in with their foolish ideas or speculations. Don't even entertain those notions. You know what you have learned by personally studying the Bible as well as attending church, Sunday school, Bible studies, and simple conversations with other mature and maturing believers (this is iron sharpening iron). You know God's truth.

You will become like him if you choose to enter this foolish conversation. That is what *not* to do. It is better not to speak than engage in foolish conversation. You are better off waiting for a more opportune time and place unless you have been in God's Word daily and are well prepared. Do your best not to think – which often leads to speech – something like, "Well, you know…" or "But…" We don't have to engage. Now, on to the second part of this passage.

Verse 5 may seem a bit twisted, but it isn't. *"Answer a fool according to his folly, lest he be wise in his own eyes."* In other words, when conversing or arguing with a "fool," answer him according to their own argument; it is appropriate to use their own words against them. We want to deconstruct - or lovingly destroy - their thought process, exposing it as folly; otherwise, they will believe they are "wise." Use their ungodly ideas and beliefs and turn them around on them. I think you'll gain some clarity as we look at four simple tests to answer the unbeliever.

Finally, remember, we are in a discussion to win people to God's Kingdom. We are not in discussion to belittle or denigrate the other person. Smile. Be thoughtful. Be courteous. Demonstrate respect, as that person is also created in the image and likeness of God.

The first test is the Folly test. These two verses from Proverbs speak to the unbeliever's folly or foolishness. The mind that has become blinded by sin will expose itself through foolish thought and speech. Do not be afraid to question the unbeliever about where they have derived their information. Test them. They should be able to prove the sense or logic of their line of thinking.

Just because it is a "popular" thought doesn't make it right. Remember when your mom would question the wisdom of your actions and ask, "If all of your friends were jumping off the Brooklyn Bridge, would you follow?" Your mom was using the test of folly. Another example: is abortion legal? Yes. Is it right or just? Why? Are they able to cogently and logically justify that answer? Don't be afraid to force the question and its response, while being respectful of the person.

One question that has been deemed very divisive in the past several years is an excellent example of a refutation of folly. It's a straightforward question that unbelievers are struggling with: "What is a woman?" That question should be straightforward to answer, yet even the most intelligent of people refuse to be honest. This question can be asked respectfully, without being snarky. It is a sincere question that should be simple to answer. Yet, certain members of our society and culture choose not to give a "binary" answer. There are many similar examples to use, which lead us to our next test.

Next is the Behavior test. The behavior test questions the unbeliever's direct behavior as it tries to "mesh" with their worldview. This test is one of the best strategies when arguing with an unbeliever. The unbeliever may have a "warped" idea of right and wrong. You know, "what's right for me may not be right for you. It's all relative." You can test them with the idea of robbing a bank or assaulting a child. If there are no standards, then what makes those wrongful acts right? Furthermore, would the particular unbeliever honestly act the way they profess? If not, then why?

These are not simply rhetorical questions.

When it comes to behavior, people do what they do and deny God in the process because they want to do what they want to do. Again, remember Romans 1:18 - 25. The unbeliever purposefully suppresses God, His Word, and His Truths to satisfy their sinfulness. The natural man doesn't want the accountability of God, ever, so that they can sin to their heart's content with little or no recourse or responsibility. Keep in mind that even we regenerated Christians struggle with accountability and sin. Even great saints like the apostle Paul struggled with sin. Paul admitted his struggle and recognized the root cause: *"I do not do the good I want, but the evil I do not want is what I keep on doing. Now if I do what I do not want, it is no longer I who do it, but sin that dwells within me."* Romans 7: 19 - 20.

The Truth test is similar to the Behavior test. Instead of "right and wrong," the question is now Truth. At Jesus' trial in front of Pontius Pilate, Pilate asks Jesus what Truth is, then quickly moves on and wishes to dismiss the charges against Him (John 18:37 - 38) without further discussion. When it comes to God, He is Truth. The "truth of the matter" is that God did create the universe in six days. It is true that Jesus was virgin born, lived a sinless life, suffered for our sins, was killed, physically died, and then bodily rose from the dead three days later. Whether you believe the truth of these facts doesn't matter. God's Truth is God's Truth. Where does the unbeliever's "truth" come from? What is their standard? Possibly, and more importantly, do they have a standard?

Here's an example: "I am created in the image of God." Genesis 1:26-27. There are two examples, really: "created" as opposed to "evolved from" and "in the image of God." As a believer, I *know* that my closest relative is not an ape or chimpanzee. There is no proof or "truth" to evolution. We stand firm on God's Word and Integrity. I believe, without question, what He has said. This now leads us to...

The Dependency test. As Bible-believing, God-loving Christians, we are 100% dependent upon God - or at least we should be. Furthermore, are we acting and living in such a way that demonstrates or expresses that dependence? On the other hand, the unbeliever wants to be 100% *independent* of God. (See the previous chapter and the discussion on the myths of Neutrality and Autonomy). They reject God in all manner of life and living. Their thinking is independent of God and the Bible. Psalm 10:13 even states that the wicked assume God won't call him to account, "Why does the wicked renounce God and say in his heart, 'You will not call to account'?" In fact, they probably won't even venture to crack a Bible's binding. And in the following sentence, they'll tell you that the Bible contains "inconsistencies" that you can't reconcile.

As believers with a good apologetic, we want to show them they can trust and depend on God. We can tell them of the actual liberty and freedom they can achieve by being dependent upon God and His Word. In this way, we can point them to the loving arms of a Saving and Personal God.

When to be careful.

Before we wrap up this chapter, let's briefly look at when we should be careful of whom we approach when speaking the Truths of God. Although Jesus has told us to go forth and spread His Gospel, the Bible is clear on whom to avoid, at least temporarily.

In the preceding section, we've already looked at "fools," but there are two other groups of individuals to be wary of: scoffers and mockers. The two groups are similar but have subtle differences, so let's define them. Scoffers are those people who are more dismissive, usually expressing disdain toward beliefs or ideas they look upon as ridiculous or unworthy of respect, such as, for example, a six-day creation, the resurrection, Jesus's second coming, or what a believer understands as a "sinful activity." Mockers, on the other hand, are those who ridicule or even taunt others to the point of using sarcasm or mimicry to make the other person appear foolish.

Let's look at several examples of what the Bible states about these two groups: *"Whoever corrects a scoffer gets himself abuse, and he who reproves a wicked man incurs injury. Do not reprove a scoffer, or he will hate you; reprove a wise man, and he will love you."* Proverbs 9:7-8

"A scoffer seeks wisdom in vain, but knowledge is easy for a man of understanding." Proverbs 14:6

"Scoffers set a city aflame, but the wise turn away wrath." Proverbs 29:8

"'Look, you scoffers, be astounded and perish; for I am doing a work in your days, a work that you will not believe, even if one tells it to you.'" Acts 13:4

"...remember the predictions of the holy prophets and the commandment of the Lord and Savior through your apostles, knowing this first of all, that scoffers will come in the last days with scoffing, following their own sinful desires. They will say, 'Where is the promise of his coming? For ever since the fathers fell asleep, all things are continuing as they were from the beginning of creation.'" 2 Peter 3:2-4

"Surely there are mockers about me, and my eye dwells on their provocation." Job 17:2

"On the day of our king, the princes became sick with the heat of wine; he stretched out his hand with mockers." Hosea 7:5

Who should we look for?

Well then, who should we be witnessing or presenting the Gospel to? The answer is that we should be looking for FAT people. FAT people are those who are Faithful, Available, and Teachable. Those we speak to should be willing to have a civil conversation, being open to God's Truths found throughout Scripture. It may even be someone that you're willing to possibly disciple. If the Lord has placed someone on our hearts to share the Gospel and the hope that is within us, we should also be willing to come alongside them to read and study the Scriptures regularly.

Most of us have not been called to be "street preachers" with a microphone at a busy intersection. But we are called to share the Gospel and "make disciples," which also means that we have to be in prayer about where and to whom God is leading us. Is it a co-worker or a family member? Perhaps it's that person sitting next to you day after day on your train commute, or the person sitting next to you on your flight to a convention or vacation.

Speaking for myself, I confess that I haven't taken full advantage of these opportunities as I should have. None of us should be shy or "ashamed" of presenting the Gospel to anyone because we know and understand its power in our lives. As we pray, God will empower us to be the witnesses He has called each of us to be. All of us can do it because when we don't have the words to speak, the Holy Spirit Himself will provide those words. Moreover, God will replace that heart of stone with a heart of flesh. What a remarkable thing!

Wrap this chapter up.

When all is said and done, we should ask ourselves: What is the purpose of constructing a "good apologetic?" If the purpose is to show our "superior" intellect or debating skills, we are being and acting selfishly. God will not honor us. If the purpose is to put the other person down or humiliate them, we are not demonstrating true Christian love and concern for their eternal soul. If we aren't regularly praying for opportunities and to share Christ, we aren't relying on Divine guidance and aid. If we aren't praying for the right words to think and speak, we are acting independently of God and, therefore, working outside His will, maybe not His direction. If, while presenting our apologetic, we cannot empathize or sympathize with the unbeliever's needs - both physical and emotional, as well as spiritual - we aren't going to be the effective guidepost that God has called us to be.

Dear friends, as we all develop and construct our apologetic, remember that this is only the first step in God's use to share Christ and further His kingdom. We should use our apologetic to show the lost their need for a personal Savior (not just an idea of God). God has called each of us to Evangelism. Therefore, you must live and work in different circumstances from those I do. God has brought every one of us to a saving faith in Him in different ways and through many different means. The believer is called to live out 1 Peter 3:15, *"...but in your hearts honor Christ the Lord as holy, always being prepared to make a defense to anyone who asks you for a reason for the hope that is in you; yet do it with gentleness and respect."*

Let us walk humbly before our God and serve Him daily for His Glory, His Honor, and His Truth.

Lesson 13 – From Doubt to Defense – Apologetic Strategies

Verses: Acts 25 – 26; Proverbs 26:4-5.

Key Questions:

How do we prepare our apologetic?
Are we completely dependent?

Paul before Festus and Agrippa (remember the noetic effects of sin – Lesson 6):

How or what does Paul say or reason when he is before Festus?

How or what does Paul say or reason when he is before Agrippa?

A Biblical Apologetic Strategy:

What NOT to do: Do not answer a fool according to his folly, or you yourself will be just like him.

What to do: Answer a fool according to his folly, or he will be wise in his own eyes.

Simple tests for the unbeliever (worldview approach – using the worldview questions):

The test of folly:

The behavior test:

The truth test:

The dependence test:

Do you know any FAT people?

Copyright© Ronald Parrs 2025

Lesson 14 – Wrapping it Up and Back to Basics

While wrapping up this study of *From Doubt to Defense*, I need to tie up a few loose ends—maybe not for you, but for myself.

Over the years of being a Christian, I have been intrigued by the intellectual arguments and discussions on Apologetics. People like John Lennox, Voddie Baucham, Frank Turek, John McArthur, Norman Geisler, Wayne Grudem, William Lane Craig, and others have tantalized my mind and, therefore, my thinking because of their eloquence and command of language skills. Not only do these men speak well, but they are all well-read; they know their stuff. They are the kind of teacher at whose feet you sit and think, "This is awesome teaching!"

But I don't believe they would think that for one minute.

And so, I sit and ponder, "So what's the point, Ron? What has got you so wrapped up in this whole Apologetics thing?"

As God allowed me to return to teaching adult Sunday school in my local church and leading (facilitating) several small-group studies, He has allowed me to expand my mind in study. The study of the Church and its influence on society and history. A study of Doctrine and the depths of our excellent Faith. The study of grace and its absolute necessity in life, living, and knowing the Mind and Heart of God. Even a Study on How to Study the Bible. I'll be honest: I have loved doing all of this sometimes for the challenge of writing and compiling a "good" Bible study.

There have been weeks where I stood in front of my peers with lesson notes in hand (the same ones included here), and I've prepared well, but something was missing. There have been other times when I felt that the preparation was mediocre, and when I opened my mouth, God was the One who put the words there; I had nothing to do with the lesson. There were some weeks - not enough of them - when God spoke a Truth through one of the class members that smote me to the core. There were weeks when I felt like our whole class was sitting at God's footstool, not because of my or my partner's preparation, but because through the entire class, God "pulled back the veil" and exposed a bit of Himself for a few moments and we were all ground to a pulp and sat amazed.

As I write these words, I am being ground down again. It's almost like the Holy Spirit is in my head and heart. He's not asking, "What's next?" He is asking me, "Do you love Me?" I feel like Peter being grilled by Jesus when he is asked, "Do you love Me?" three times.

"When they had finished breakfast, Jesus said to Simon Peter, 'Simon, son of John, do you love me more than these?' He said to him, 'Yes, Lord; you know that I love you.' He said to him, 'Feed my lambs.' He said to him a second time, 'Simon, son of John, do you love me?' He said to him, 'Yes, Lord; you know that I love you.' He said to him, 'Tend my sheep.' He said to him the third time, 'Simon, son of John, do you love me?' Peter was grieved because he said to him the third time, 'Do you love me?' and he said to him, 'Lord, you know everything; you know that I love you.' Jesus said to him, 'Feed my sheep. Truly, truly, I say to you, when you were young, you used to dress yourself and walk wherever you wanted, but when you are old, you will stretch out your hands, and another will dress you and carry you where you do not want to go.' This he said to show by what kind of death he was to glorify God. And after saying this he said to him, 'Follow me.'

[Later] *"Peter turned and saw the disciple whom Jesus loved following them, the one who also had leaned back against him during the supper and had said, 'Lord, who is it that is going to betray you?' When Peter saw him, he said to Jesus, 'Lord, what about this man?' Jesus said to him, 'If it is my will that he remain until I come, what is that to you? You follow me!'"* John 21:15-22

Peter answers "yes" at each moment, and the Lord is just making sure that this beloved disciple, soon to be an apostle, gets the real meaning of what the Savior asks. Jesus admonishes Peter not to worry about what will happen to John; that's His responsibility. Peter had his orders. Like Peter, we must be concerned with what God has asked us to do individually. Almost more importantly, I'm not to worry about anybody else's testimony or apologetic except my own. As God dealt with me, He will deal with His other children as He will.

Through all of these studies and the time spent in various books, study guides, and materials, I have gained much knowledge about the topics at hand. But now, as this study of apologetics has been put to bed, I am again crushed by God. God has crushed me because He has reminded me that it's not about the study. It's not about the topic or the knowledge gained. It's not about constructing a good or worthy apologetic that "destroys" an unbeliever's folly. It is about making sure that my Bible is being opened every single day out of love and spending time in prayer with my Creator. In short, it IS about God.

Two concluding thoughts come to mind as we wrap up this study. First, everything is about God. No matter what, it's all about Him. Do I—do you—love God with all of my body, soul, heart, and mind? Do I—do you—love God so much that all else is rubbish?

Second of all—a really close second—I am compelled to give a reason for my hope to the people I love that God has placed in my sphere of influence, as Peter has admonished. *"Always be prepared to make a defense to anyone who asks you for a reason for the hope that is in you; [and] do it with gentleness and respect."* 1 Peter 3:15.

Will I hide in my study with my books, Bible, and laptop, learning all there is to know about God? Or will I rend my heart and mind and begin to allow Him to have control over all of my thoughts, words, and deeds? For me, that's where the rubber meets the road. If I am willing to allow God that access, then I am in for a radical change. I will allow God to use me willingly, or I will force Him out and not participate in what He wants to accomplish.

As I look at my mentors, Paul, Peter, Piper, Lennox, Sproul, McArthur, Borgman, McIntyre, Roy, Craddock, Driver, Matthews, Sampson, and many others, past and present, I realize that the most important thing that all of these men have are two things that I often lack: an unbridled zeal for God coupled with a passion for the unsaved. These men (and a few women too) are passionate for the Savior as well as compassionate for the people around them. They love God so much that they want to ensure that as many people come to a saving knowledge of Jesus Christ as possible in the limited time God has given them.

So, in closing, I ask you, please think about this: Why are you studying God's Word or Apologetics or Doctrine? If it's to be smart or gain enough head knowledge to win a debate against an atheist, so what? You will have gained NOTHING. But if it's to know God better or to walk closer with your Creator, you are stepping in the right direction. If it's to want to be used by God to win souls and a great harvest, then I think He has your attention.

We live in challenging yet exciting times. God wants to use all of His children every day for great things in finishing His work of redemption. He is planning and preparing a great Harvest and wants all of us to participate.

Thank you for your time and be a blessing to all.

Lesson 14 - From Doubt to Defense – Wrapping it up & Back to Basics!

Verses: 1 Peter 3:15 – 16

Key Questions:

How do we prepare our apologetic?

Are we completely dependent?

Primary Strategies:

1.

2.

3.

4.

5.

Two final questions:

1. What is God asking of YOU?

2. What is your response?

Copyright© Ronald Parrs 2025

Key Verses & Passages

1 Peter 3:13-17

¹³ Now who is there to harm you if you are zealous for what is good? ¹⁴ But even if you should suffer for righteousness' sake, you will be blessed. Have no fear of them, nor be troubled, ¹⁵ but in your hearts honor Christ the Lord as holy, always being prepared to make a defense to anyone who asks you for a reason for the hope that is in you; yet do it with gentleness and respect, ¹⁶ having a good conscience, so that, when you are slandered, those who revile your good behavior in Christ may be put to shame. ¹⁷ For it is better to suffer for doing good, if that should be God's will, than for doing evil.

2 Peter 3:14-18

¹⁴ Therefore, beloved, since you are waiting for these, be diligent to be found by him without spot or blemish, and at peace. ¹⁵ And count the patience of our Lord as salvation, just as our beloved brother Paul also wrote to you according to the wisdom given him, ¹⁶ as he does in all his letters when he speaks in them of these matters. There are some things in them that are hard to understand, which the ignorant and unstable twist to their own destruction, as they do the other Scriptures. ¹⁷ You therefore, beloved, knowing this beforehand, take care that you are not carried away with the error of lawless people and lose your own stability. ¹⁸ But grow in the grace and knowledge of our Lord and Savior Jesus Christ. To him be the glory both now and to the day of eternity. Amen.

Romans 1:18-32

¹⁸ For the wrath of God is revealed from heaven against all ungodliness and unrighteousness of men, who by their unrighteousness suppress the truth. ¹⁹ For what can be known about God is plain to them, because God has shown it to them. ²⁰ For his invisible attributes, namely, his eternal power and divine nature, have been clearly perceived, ever since the creation of the world, in the things that have been made. So they are without excuse. ²¹ For although they knew God, they did not honor him as God or give thanks to him, but they became futile in their thinking, and their foolish hearts were darkened. ²² Claiming to be wise, they became fools,

²³ and exchanged the glory of the immortal God for images resembling mortal man and birds and animals and creeping things.

²⁴ Therefore God gave them up in the lusts of their hearts to impurity, to the dishonoring of their bodies among themselves, ²⁵ because they exchanged the truth about God for a lie and worshiped and served the creature rather than the Creator, who is blessed forever! Amen.

²⁶ For this reason God gave them up to dishonorable passions. For their women exchanged natural relations for those that are contrary to nature; ²⁷ and the men likewise gave up natural relations with women and were consumed with passion for one another, men committing shameless acts with men and receiving in themselves the due penalty for their error.

²⁸ And since they did not see fit to acknowledge God, God gave them up to a debased mind to do what ought not to be done. ²⁹ They were filled with all manner of unrighteousness, evil, covetousness, malice. They are full of envy, murder, strife, deceit, maliciousness. They are gossips, ³⁰ slanderers, haters of God, insolent, haughty, boastful, inventors of evil, disobedient to parents, ³¹ foolish, faithless, heartless, ruthless. ³² Though they know God's righteous decree that those who practice such things deserve to die, they not only do them but give approval to those who practice them.

Romans 8:7 - 8

⁷ For the mind that is set on the flesh is hostile to God, for it does not submit to God's law; indeed, it cannot. ⁸ Those who are in the flesh cannot please God.

Proverbs 26:4 - 5

⁴ Answer not a fool according to his folly,
   lest you be like him yourself.
⁵ Answer a fool according to his folly,
   lest he be wise in his own eyes.

Resources

Apologetics is not so much about "technique" as about being firmly grounded in Holy Scripture. Christians are obligated to become as mature as possible in their faith. Why? Why not? If you're in a personal relationship with someone, don't you want to know and understand the other person well to have and develop a strong and long-lasting relationship?

We come to better know God by reading and studying His Word directly. Without daily Bible reading and study, books about God are fairly ineffective. As much as possible, God wants us to not only become "experts" on Him and Who He is, but He wants us to know Him intimately. Our relationship with God should be the most intimate one we can ever have.

In my opinion, only after we have become regular students and lovers of the Bible should we delve into other books and resources about God, Jesus Christ, the Holy Spirit, the Gospel and other Bible based Christian doctrine. With that in mind, I offer the following resources to you in understanding your own faith and personal relationship with God as well as the study of Apologetics. I have found each of these books very helpful, not only in understanding my faith, but also in communicating with others as well.

"Every Thought Captive", Richard L. Pratt, a study manual for the defense of the Christian Truth. A relatively short and simple (easy to read as well as understand) book (originally written for teens) on the basics of Christian apologetics. Great for Sunday school, small group or personal study. ISBN-10: 0-87552-352-8

"Apologetics to the Glory of God", John M. Frame. John Frame believes in going on the offensive when it comes to apologetics. Sometimes the other side doesn't play "nice" and we Christians shouldn't be doormats. It is our responsibility to offer reasons, proofs, and evidences to our faith using Scripture as our only authority. An excellent resource. ISBN: 978-0-87552-243-2

"The Universe Next Door", James W. Sire, a basic worldview catalog. Fifth edition. In order to present our Christian apologetic, we need to understand the mind and mindset of our audience. Sire presents in clear and readable format the worldviews of other belief systems, both theistic and non-theistic. If you teach or regularly engage non-believers, then you need to know what and how they think. This book should be on your bookshelf. ISBN: 978-0-8308-3850-9

"The Case for Easter", Lee Strobel. All of the "Case for..." books by Lee Strobel are excellent, but this is my favorite because our faith, the Christian faith, hinges on the actual and historical death, burial, and resurrection of Jesus Christ, and without it, our faith is nothing. Strobel was an ardent unbeliever that chose to explore Christianity and its claims in an honest way. In time, he came to saving knowledge of Christ. Short and easy to read. ISNB: 0-310-25475-2

"The Reason for God", Timothy Keller, belief in an Age of Skepticism. A favorite book of mine because it presents the thoughts and ideas of the unbelievers in their own words. Once we understand them, we are better able to engage in a thoughtful conversation which can lead to the saving of souls through the power of God. ISBN: 978-1-59448-349-3

"Systematic Theology, Second Edition: An Introduction to Biblical Doctrine", Wayne A. Grudem, an absolute must have on your study shelf. In this second edition, Grudem in a concise manner, expands his painstaking reviews of the doctrines of our faith in 57 chapters. ISBN: 978-0-3105-1797-9

"Systematic Theology: In One Volume," Norman L. Geisler. Another must have book for your study shelf. The one-volume editions are a slightly abridged amalgamation of Norm's earlier (2002-2005) four-volume set of Systematic Theology. ISBN: 978-1737654605

"Living by the Book", Howard G. Hendricks, William D. Hendricks. My favorite book when I want to teach someone how to read and study the Bible. Another must have for your study shelf. ISBN 10: 0802408168

Appendix – Study Leader Notes

Below are notes for those who, as God leads, will lead this study in their Sunday School class or small group. Each lesson note provides additional space for you to fill in your thoughts as you study and search the Scriptures in preparation for leading your group. As a leader, you should spend time reading, studying God's Word and other reference sources, and praying in preparation for your time with the group. As a leader, God expects more from you in terms of time, commitment, and grace to disciple others.

The font used in the leader notes is LARGER for teaching from a podium, making them easier to read. There is also room on each page for your notes and thoughts.

Occasionally, Bible verses are mentioned in the lessons, but they are not quoted. I encourage you, the leader, to look up these verses yourself and your students so that you can read and understand these complementary concepts as well.

As a leader, our job is to guide our group in thought, discussion, and prayer. The Word of God, like the Holy Spirit, is the teacher.

There are many people around the world praying for you and the group God has given you. Let's get going with God's leading!

Leader Notes: Lesson 1 – From Doubt to Defense – Defining Your World View – Three Fundamental Questions

Question One: Who is God? Part 1

Verses: Genesis 1:1, 26, Job 38, Mark 1:9-11

Key Questions:

What is the difference between "theism" and Christian theism?

Why is it important to understand the difference?

The Christian understanding of God: Christian Theism and the Triunity of God

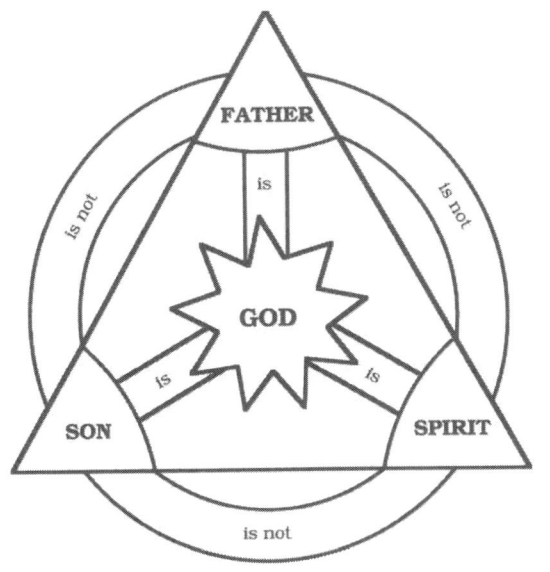

The members of the Holy Trinity are United, Distinct, and Equal

"Trinity" is NOT mentioned in the Bible

The Trinity is NOT 3 gods

The Incommunicable "O's" & "I's" of God:

What is the difference between "communicable" & "incommunicable"? Define the differences.

God's un- or not shared attributes. These attributes are not shared with any created being.

Omnipotent – all powerful;
don't buy into the straw man of God creating a rock He couldn't lift

a straw man or straw man argument – a deceptive tactic to take you off-point.

What things has God done to demonstrate His omnipotence in History and in your own life?

Omnipresent – all present;
know the beginning from the end & the middle

What things has God done to demonstrate His omnipresence in History and in your own life?

Omniscient – all knowing; there is nothing that He does not know

Recall a time in your own life when you realized that God knew what He was doing? Details.

Omnisapient – all wise; everything that He does is with perfect wisdom

Recall a time when you realized God's omnisapience in your own life.

Immutable – un or never changing; God doesn't "change" His mind

Why do we rely on God's immutability?

Independent – self-sustaining

Why is God's independence important to us?

Infinite – eternal; always was, is & will be

Why is God's eternity important to us?

Indivisible – cannot be divided or broken down into parts; the members of the Trinity are of One Essence; the Trinity works as a whole

Each of the above incommunicable attributes speak and contribute to God's:

Sovereignty – He is the absolute & only ruler of the Universe whether seen or unseen, natural or supernatural. Everything was & is made for Him & for His honor & glory

Why is God's sovereignty important in your own life?

Copyright© Ronald Parrs 2025

Leader Notes: Lesson 2 – From Doubt to Defense – Defining Your World View – Three Fundamental Questions

Question One: Who is God? Part 2

Is Christianity Monotheistic in Nature? Why?

The Trinity
There exists ONE God in 3 Persons
The "Godhead" consists of:

1. **Essence** – the key characteristics that make God, God

    Eternal – has always existed; never didn't exist

    Essential – nothing exists or can exist without God

    Equal – equally omniscient, equally omnipotent, equally omnipresent

2. **Person** – the "Roles" or "Functions" of the Persons of the Deity are

    God the Father chooses

    God the Son redeems man to Himself

    God the Holy Spirit seals or puts His mark on the redeemed

relationship best described in Ephesians 1:1-14

What distinguishes God from everything else in all of Creation? Some of God's attributes are "communicable" (transferable to man – example: "graciousness" – when man wants to be gracious) others are "incommunicable" (example – God's holiness).

We believe yet don't understand!

The Attributes & Functions of God

God the Father

Attributes	Roles or Actions
Eternal	Chooses – Ephesians 1
Self-sufficient - Aseity	Sends forth Jesus and the Holy Spirit – Romans 3:23,
Essential	
Immutable	Creates – Genesis 1
Omniscient, Omnisapient	
Omnipotent	Ruler of Heaven & Earth – Matthew 11:25
Omnipresent	
Holy *	
Just *	
Righteous *	
Wise *	
Good	
Severe *	
Wrath *	
Love *	
Judge *	
Truth *	
Jealous *	
Sovereign	
Gracious *, Spiritual *	
Perfect *, Majestic *, Forgives *, Mercy *	

God the Son

Attributes	Roles or Actions
See above	Creates – John 1:3
	Preserves or Sustains – Hebrews 1:3, Colossians 1:17
	Judges – John 5:22, 8:16
	Reflects the Father – Hebrews 1:3
	Redeems – Galatians 3:13
	Miracles - Gospels

God the Holy Spirit

Attributes	Roles or Actions
See above	Speaks – Mark 13:11, Acts 13:2
	Instructs – Neh. 9:20, John 14:2, 6
	Intercedes – Romans 8:26
	Gives spiritual life – John 6:63
	Inspires Scripture – 2 Timothy 3:16
	Convicts man of sin – John 16:7-8
	Indwells believers – John 14:17, Romans 8:9, 1 Corinthians 6:19

Similarities:

Differences:

The attributes marked with an asterisk are communicable.

Leader Notes: Lesson 3 – From Doubt to Defense – Getting Started Requires a Good Start

Verses: 1 Peter 3:15 – 16, 2 Peter 3:15 – 18 & Acts 1:1 - 11

Key Questions:

What is the study of Apologetics and why is it necessary?

What and How does God teach us about apologetics?

Apologetics: the presentation of a good defense of an idea or cause or doctrine

Why discuss Apologetics? 1 Peter 3:15 – 16, 2 Peter 3:15 – 18

What is the purpose in understanding, discussing, and constructing a personal apologetic?

The Basics of Apologetics: Acts 1:1 – 11

What strikes you most from this passage?

The entire Godhead teaches us: Father, Son, and Holy Spirit.

The work of the Holy Spirit: v. 2

The work of the Son: v. 3 – 5. How and what does Jesus do to instruct us in the work of Apologetics?

1. V 3 – Show up; take advantage of situations

   Do you purposefully place yourself in positions of help or assistance where you may be able to open a conversation?

   Who do you regularly "hang out" with?

   Who is in "sphere of influence"?

2. V 3 – Speak; be willing to open your mouth. God will speak for you when necessary

   When provided the opportunity, do you take advantage of that opportunity?

Why?

Why not?

3. V 4 – Command or share scripture or a Biblical truth. People are looking for absolutes

   Do you have certain or particular passages of Scripture memorized or at least well paraphrased and know where you can find them for context in the Bible? Speciifically

   Do you understand or have a rudimentary grasp of the passage of Scripture to better explain it?

   This means that you have to be in God's Word on a daily basis.

The work of the Father: the entire passage. The Father is behind every aspect.

Copyright© Ronald Parrs 2025

Leader Notes: Lesson 4 – From Doubt to Defense – Speaking in Tongues

Verses: Acts 2:1 – 12

Key Questions:

What is the work of the Holy Spirit in our lives?

Are we speaking in "tongues" that our society can hear and understand?

Tongues: the presentation of the Gospel of Jesus Christ using words that the hearer will hear, listen to, understand

What do we have to do to allow the Holy Spirit to work in our lives? Acts 2:1 – 4

What are "other tongues" in today's society? Acts 2: 6 – 11

Home

School

Workplace

Grocery store

House party

What other examples can you think of when you need to speak in "another tongue"?

What are we speaking about when we talk to people in the world around us? Acts 2:11

Leader's Notes: Lesson 5 – From Doubt to Defense – Peter's Keys to Apologetics

Verses: Acts 2:14 – 41, Joel 2:12 – 13, 32

Key Questions:

How does God use "ordinary" people?

What does God expect of us?

Peter's Model: the "model" presented in Acts 2 demonstrating 5 keys to Apologetics

Why the Old Testament? Joel 2:12 – 13, 32. The relevancy of Old Testament passages. Discuss your gleanings from this passage in the section below.

Peter's 5 Keys to Apologetics Acts 2: 14 – 41

1. Stand with your brothers and sisters in Christ - verse 14

What does it mean to stand with fellow Christians?

2. Know God's Word – verses 17 – 21, 25 – 28, 34 - 35

Who is Peter quoting in these verses?

3. Acknowledge God – verses 14 - 41

How is God acknowledged?

4. Acknowledge Jesus Christ – verses 22 - 24

In what ways is Jesus acknowledged?

5. Acknowledge Our Need – verses 37 – 41

What is our need and why do we need to acknowledge it?

How are we incorporating these 5 keys when we talk to people in the world around us?

Copyright© Ronald Parrs 2025

Leader Notes: Lesson 6 – From Doubt to Defense – Practical Preaching

Verses: Acts 2:42 – 47

Key Questions:

How do we "walk the walk"?

How do we "talk the talk"?

How do we walk and talk?

As you look at Acts 2:42 – 47, discuss the how the 3 general "Walks" were accomplished.

1. Devotion -
a. to God

b. to our Church leaders

c. to one another

2. Giving -
a. to God

b. to our Church leaders

c. to one another

3. Praise -
a. personal life

b. public life

The Foundation: How are you making the Bible your firm foundation?

Copyright© Ronald Parrs 2025

Leader Notes: Lesson 7 – From Doubt to Defense – Right Relationship

Verses: Genesis 1 – 2, Hebrews 11:6

Without a proper understanding of Who God is and who we are, it is impossible to form a correct defense of the Gospel. In this present day, Christians are truly running countercultural.

We need a foundational understanding of how we are to relate to God and how He relates to man.

Key Questions:

What does the Bible assert about God?

Is God revealing Himself today?

Creator vs. Creature
God's Independence –

Job 38 – 39 – Review God's questioning of Job

Man's Dependence –

1. Physical Dependence

Psalm 139:13–16

2. Historical Dependence

Romans 15:4, Acts 7

3. Knowledge

a. General revelation – define this term
Psalm 19:1

b. Special revelation - define this term
Hebrews 1:1–2 , John 6:44–51

4. Morality

Psalm 119

How would you sum up or put into perspective this Creator - Creature relationship to an unbeliever?

Leader Notes: Lesson 8 – From Doubt to Defense – The Sin Problem

Verses: Acts 7, Psalm 10:2-11

Key Questions:

What is sin?
What are the "noetic" effects of sin?

Define Sin in your own words:

What was man like before the Fall?

Effects of Sin as it relates to:

God

Our Society

Culture in General

Our Personal Lives

The Noetic effects of Sin (look up Biblical references):

Define "noetic effects" for your group

1. Stubbornness

2. Enmity against God

3. Seared conscience or hardened heart

4. Arrogance

5. Spiritual death

6. Foolishness

7. Empty reasoning or darkened understanding

8. Others?

How do the noetic effects of sin play into apologetics?

Leader Notes: Lesson 9 – From Doubt to Defense – The Redemption Solution

Verses: Romans 12:1-2, Acts 8

Key Questions:

What is redemption?
Why does redemption begin in the mind? – We must desire redemption in order to be redeemed.

Define Redemption in your own words:

What is the Redemption process?

Reversing the Fall:

How

The Effects

Restoration by Regeneration:

How

The Effects

The Responsibilities

Redemption vs. Sanctification

Why? – What is the difference between Redemption and Sanctification?

What about Spirituality?

Leader Notes: Lesson 10 – From Doubt to Defense – The Christian Worldview

Verses: Romans 12:1-2, Acts 9

Key Questions:

What is a worldview?
Can a person's worldview change or be changed?

Facts are interpreted by our worldview.

A person's Worldview is made of how we view the world around us. We look at the world around us by answering the questions: "What is the Nature of…"

Define each of the following terms in your own words and describe how you would apply it.

1. Ontology

2. Cosmology

3. Anthropology

4. Epistemology

5. Ethics

6. Teleology

7. Commitment

How did Paul's Worldview change?

What is your worldview?

How has your worldview changed? – Especially after your salvation experience.

How would you express your worldview to a "seeker"?

Copyright© Ronald Parrs 2025

Leader Notes: Lesson 11 – From Doubt to Defense – The Unbeliever's Worldview

Verses: Romans 1:18 – 23, Acts 17:13 – 34

Key Questions:

How do Christian and non-Christian worldviews differ?

Can a person's worldview change or be changed?

Facts are interpreted by our worldview.

What were the beliefs of the Epicureans and Stoics of first-century Athens?

Epicureans –

Stoics -

A person's Worldview is made up of how we view the world around us. We look at the world around us by answering the questions: "What is the Nature of…"

1. Ontology

2. Cosmology

3. Anthropology

4. Epistemology

5. Ethics

6. Teleology (purpose)

8. Commitment

If "chance" and "chaos" is the basis of the unbeliever's worldview, are they able to live out these worldview ideas?

Copyright© Ronald Parrs 2025

Leader Notes: Lesson 12 – From Doubt to Defense - Actions and Attitudes

Verses: 1 Peter 3:15, Acts 11:1-18; 17:1-9; 23:1-10; 24:24-27.

Key Questions:

Can we be neutral or autonomous in our thought?
How are we to present our Apologetic?

Myths.

Neutrality –

Autonomy -

Attitude check: My attitude determines my personal Apologetic.

How has your attitude changed through this study?

How has your attitude affected your walk with God?

What further changes would you like to see?

How does your attitude affect unbelievers?

Copyright© Ronald Parrs 2025

Leader Notes: Lesson 13 – From Doubt to Defense - Your Apologetic

Verses: Acts 25 – 26; Proverbs 26:4-5.

Key Questions:

How do we prepare our apologetic?

Are we completely dependent?

Paul before Festus and Agrippa (remember the noetic effects of sin – Lesson 6): What is Paul's attitude toward Festus, Agrippa, their wives and anyone in attendance?

How or what does Paul say or reason when he is before Festus?

– Festus is a Roman and, therefore, a Gentile.

How or what does Paul say or reason when he is before Agrippa?

– Agrippa is a Jewish leader

Why is it necessary to address these men individually?

A Biblical Apologetic Strategy:

What NOT to do: Do not answer a fool according to his folly, or you yourself will be just like him.

What to do: Answer a fool according to his folly, or he will be wise in his own eyes.

Simple tests for the unbeliever (worldview approach – using the worldview questions):

The test of folly:

The behavior test:

The truth test:

The dependence test:

Do you know any FAT people?

Faithful

Available

Teachable

Copyright© Ronald Parrs 2025

Leader Notes: Lesson 14 - From Doubt to Defense – Wrapping up and Back to Basics!

Verses: 1 Peter 3:15 – 16

Key Questions:

How do we prepare our apologetic?

Are we completely dependent?

Primary Strategies:

1.

2.

3.

4.

5.

Two final questions:

1. What is God asking of YOU?

2. What is your response?

Copyright© Ronald Parrs 2025

Made in the USA
Middletown, DE
25 November 2025